O My Hornby and My Barlow Long Ago

The Life of the Poet Francis Thompson 1859-1907

Kenneth Shenton

Max Books

First published in the UK in 2019 by Max Books

A CIP catalogue record for this title is available from the British Library

ISBN: 978-0-9934872-6-2

Typeset and Design by Andrew Searle

Printed and bound by in India

MAX BOOKS
2 Newbold Way
Nantwich
CW5 7AX
Email: maxcricket@btinternet.com
www.max-books.co.uk

Dedicated to the memory of my late father,

A TRUE DABBER,

Who spent countless years during his youth frequenting Kingsley Fields.

His many tales of cricketing heroes past, most notably the memorable exploits of such as Albert Neilson Hornby, lie at the very heart of this volume.

Contents

Contents

Acknowledgements

Of those numerous institutions consulted, I would particularly like to thank The Bodleian Library in Oxford: Boston College, Chestnut Hill, Massachusetts; Harris Library in Preston; Harrow School; the John Rylands Library at the University of Manchester; University of Durham Library and the Special Collections, Manchester Metropolitan University. At the College of St Cuthbert, Ushaw, County Durham, may I express special thanks to the Curator, Claire Marsland.

Among the musical fraternity, never slow to respond to my many enquiries were the staff of music publishers: Stainer and Bell; Royal College of Music; Royal School of Church Music; Julian Jacobson; and composers Howard Blake, Ronald Corp and Paul Spicer, together with everyone at Highbridge Music, London. Thanks to all for the supply not only of information and encouragement but also their generosity in providing musical scores.

To those pioneers who, over the last century have written with such skill and expertise on Francis Thompson, and hopefully have inspired me to do the same. They include June Badeni, Brigid Boardman, Peter Butter, Father Terence Connolly, Pierre Danchin, Ifor Evans, Holbrook Jackson, Francis Noel Lees, Rodolphe Mégroz, Everard Meynell, Sir Francis Meynell, Viola Meynell, John Reid, John Thomson, Paul van Kuykendall Thomson and John Walsh. Grateful thanks are also due to Oliver Hawkins for permission to use documents and photographic material from the Meynell Family Papers.

As I prepared this volume, I became increasingly aware of, and highly appreciative of the many qualities of the writer, Edward Verrall Lucas, not least his articulate advocacy and championing of Francis Thompson's cricket poetry. Like Thompson, more a connoisseur than a successful participant, nevertheless Lucas' writing remains both evocative and unfailingly nostalgic. Similarly, he too never seemed happier than when mourning his countless cricketing heroes.

Particular thanks are due to Ken Grime for his help in both proof reading and indexing and my publisher, Rev. Malcolm Lorimer for his help and good counsel. For many years Malcolm has combined the roles of local cleric, historian and archivist at Lancashire County Cricket Club with such aplomb. Here also mention should be made of the expertise and knowledge of the late Don Ambrose, who devoted so much time and effort to uncovering and revealing the past glories of all those who have trodden the hallowed turf of Old Trafford. Heartiest thanks are also due to the writer, Michael Henderson, for his most erudite foreword.

Likewise too, the staff at my local library. No request, no matter how obscure was ever too much trouble. For me, not living in London, the inter-library loan system often proved a particular life saver.

Never slow to offer her expertise and advice, I thank my eldest daughter, Sarah. Her dogged research capabilities and, not least, her computer skills proved invaluable in the compilation of this volume.

Thanks are also due to my long-suffering wife, Karen, for her endless patience, while I shared my life with such a demanding subject. She has now taken charge once more of our dining room.

Alas, all the imperfections in this volume remain mine.

Kenneth Shenton

Foreword

by Michael Henderson

Francis Thompson is one of the most remarkable figures of the Victorian age. Perhaps it would be more truthful to call him a phenomenon. Marked down as a doctor by his parents, he went through the necessary medical training before deciding, at the age of 26, that his calling was poetry, for which he gave his life.

Unable to support himself when he moved to London, where he lived on the streets, he turned increasingly to opium. A fragile soul, essentially one of life's misfits, he found a refuge in poetry that was not there in his daily life, and though his work was largely unappreciated in his lifetime it has found readers since his death.

In this country he is best-known for the elegiac At Lord's, in which he fondly recalls through eyes misty with tears Hornby and Barlow, the Lancashire batsmen of his childhood. It is an evocation of cricket, and of that 'land of lost content' described by another poet, AE Housman, which cannot come again. In America, however, his religious imagery has found favour as a branch of Catholic mysticism. The Hound of Heaven in particular is regarded as one of the most significant poems of the 19th century.

Kenneth Shenton, cricket-lover and schoolmaster, has shed light on the odd case of this singular man, troubled in life yet triumphant in his afterlife. He deserves our commendation.

Introduction

2019 marks the 160th anniversary of the birth of the once celebrated, but now sadly neglected Preston born poet, Francis Thompson. During his short yet highly eventful life, perhaps no writer has suffered more for his art. A devout Roman Catholic, having trained for the priesthood, enduring indolence judged him unsuitable for ordination. He subsequently failed his medical examinations on numerous occasions and was finally rejected as a soldier. Following a family argument, he left home to try and earn a living as a writer in London. Having already fallen prey to opium addiction, he followed the path prescribed by an earlier Lancastrian, Thomas de Quincey, who himself died in the very year that Thompson was born.

Initially forced to live on the capital's streets as a destitute vagrant, the poet found himself, pitched betwixt Heaven and Charing Cross. Befriended by a prostitute, on more than one occasion, he even became a major suspect in the Jack the Ripper murders. However, thanks to the support of the publisher, Wilfrid Meynell, Thompson's extensive output of poetry and literary criticism eventually began to be published in the latter years of the nineteenth century. Central to that creative output was his Catholic faith, which he held so humbly and yet embellished so royally. Ignored in life and little mourned in death, his message has possibly had to wait for a future age to be more widely understood and appreciated.

It was exactly one hundred years ago that a young British composer, William Harris, won a prestigious Carnegie Award for his setting for Baritone, Chorus and Orchestra of Francis Thompson's most famous creation, *The Hound of Heaven*. It is a stunning work, and though now rarely performed, it remains one of the major choral masterpieces of 20th Century British music. In its day it inspired a number of fellow composers to follow suit and add their own highly distinctive musical vision to Thompson's poetry. However, it has not only been musicians who have been stimulated by the poet's unique outlook. As this volume relates, numerous other artists, writers and playwrights have also eagerly taken up the challenge.

Alongside his faith, Thompson never lost his enduring fascination with the game of cricket. As a youth, having spent endless hours watching his native county play at Old Trafford when he should have been studying, he later seriously contemplated writing a volume on the history of the game. Though rarely feeling able to watch the game in later life, nevertheless he remained an astute observer. Following his death, the averages of his many cricketing heroes, most carefully compiled over the course of more than thirty years, were found among his papers. Accompanying them were numerous unpublished cricketing verses, some of which unfailingly draw the reader into a shared discourse of English remembrance.

By yet a further coincidence, 2019 marks the centenary of the death of one of Thompson's greatest idols, the renowned Lancashire and England cricketer, Richard Gorton Barlow. However, when writing about this veteran of forty seasons of first class cricket, it proved impossible to ignore his opening partner and fellow run-stealer, *The Boss*, Albert Neilson Hornby. Now thanks to Thompson, they are irretrievably linked, just as Gilbert and Sullivan go so effortlessly together within English opera. Hornby, the sprightly Cavalier amateur, careless of risk and carefree in assault, had genius, and if he very well knew it, he didn't really care. Barlow, the Roundhead professional, had skill, increasing his early talent into untold riches.

Only a poet of rare and undoubted vision could have united them in such a memorable and moving way:

AT LORD'S

It is little I repair to the matches of the Southron folk,
        Though my own red roses there may blow;
It is little I repair to the matches of the Southron folk,
        Though the red roses crest the caps I know.
For the field is full of shades as I near the shadowy coast,
And a ghostly batsman plays to the bowling of a ghost,
And I look through my tears on a soundless clapping host,
        As the run-stealers flicker to and fro,
                To and fro:-
        O my Hornby and my Barlow long ago!

It is Glo'ster coming North, the irresistible,
        The Sire of the Graces, long ago!
It is Gloucestershire up North, the irresistible,
        And new-arisen Lancashire the foe!
A Shire so young that has scarce impressed its traces,
Ah, how shall it stand before all resistless Graces?
O little red rose, their bats are as maces
        To beat thee down, this summer long ago!

This day of seventy-eight they are come up North against thee,
        This day of seventy-eight, long ago!
The champion of the centuries, he cometh up against thee,
        With his brethren, every one a famous foe!
The long-whiskered Doctor, that laugheth rules to scorn,
While the bowler, pitched against him, bans the day that he was born;
And G.F. with his science makes the fairest length forlorn;
        They are come up from the West to work thee woe!

It is little I repair to the matches of the Southron folk,
        Though my own red roses there may blow;
It is little I repair to the matches of the Southron folk,
        Though the red roses crest the caps I know.
For the field is full of shades as I near the shadowy coast,
And a ghostly batsman plays to the bowling of a ghost,
And I look through my tears on a soundless clapping host,
        As the run-stealers flicker to and fro,
                To and fro:-
        O my Hornby and my Barlow long ago!

CHRONOLOGY

1859 On 18th December Francis Joseph Thompson, born a Roman Catholic at Preston in Lancashire. Only surviving son of a homeopathic doctor.

1864 Family moves to Ashton-under-Lyne.

1870 Becomes a student at Ushaw College, Durham.

1877 Rejected for the priesthood.

1878 Enrols as a medical student at Manchester Royal Infirmary.

1879 Mother gives him a copy of the *Confessions Of An English Opium Eater* by Thomas De Quincey.

1885 Moves away from home after a family argument to live in London.

1887 First meeting with Wilfrid and Alice Meynell.

1888 First published poem - *The Passion Of Mary* appears in *Merry England.*

1889 Sent to live at the Premonstratensian Priory, Storrington, Sussex.

1890 Returns to London. *The Hound of Heaven* first published in *Merry England.*

1892 Moves to live at the Capuchin Monastery at Pantasaph, North Wales.

1893 First collection of poetry – *Poems* published by Elkin Matthews and John Lane.

1894 Meets the poet, Coventry Patmore.

1895 Thompson's second collection of poetry – *Sister Songs* published by Elkin Matthews and John Lane.

1897 Third collection – *New Poems*, published by Constable and Son. Thompson returns to live in London.

1907 On 13th November, Thompson dies aged 47. Buried at Kensal Green Cemetery, London.

1908 Cricket poetry first published in an article by E. V. Lucas in *The Cornhill Magazine*.

1913 Three volume edition of Thompson's poetry published, edited by Wilfrid Meynell, Thompson's literary executor.

1922 Death of Alice Meynell. Buried at Kensal Green Cemetery.

1932 *Poems of Francis Thompson* published. Edited by Father Terence Connolly.

1948 Death of Wilfrid Meynell, aged 96.

Chapter 1

EARLY DAYS

> I was born in 1858 or 1859 (I could never remember and don't care which) at Preston in Lancashire. Residing there, my mother more than once pointed out to me, as we passed it, the house wherein I was born; and it seemed to me disappointingly like any other house.[1]

Everard Meynell's pioneering biography of the poet opens with the above quotation from Francis Thompson himself. While he remains somewhat vague about his date of birth, there can be no doubt about the place. Preston itself occupies the northern banks of the River Ribble, at the very heart of Lancashire and close to the centre of the British Isles. In medieval times, when cloisters were as numerous as factories, it was known as Preostatum, the Priests' town. Its famous Charter, granted by Henry II in 1179, allowed the inhabitants a civic celebration every twenty years, giving rise to the famous saying, *Once Every Preston Guild.*

Initially a small market town, by the time the Thompson family arrived, it had long lost any vestige of medieval charm. Then its bustling docks, ship building industry, countless foundries, mills and factories increasingly dominated the vast industrial landscape. Remaining very much at the forefront of the Industrial Revolution, it was thanks to the likes of local entrepreneurs John Horrocks and Richard Arkwright, that Preston developed into one of the county's leading industrial centres. In the thirty years from 1831 to 1861, its population rose quickly from 33,112 to 82,985.[2] With such rapid expansion however, came a whole host of social problems and unrest. Poverty was severe, and in the Guild Year of 1842, four people were killed in civil disturbances that took place in Lune Street.[3]

> It was a town of red brick, or of brick that would have been red if the smoke and ashes allowed it; but as matters stood it was a town of unnatural red and black like the painted face of a savage. It was a town of machinery and tall chimneys, out of which interminable serpents of smoke trailed themselves for ever and ever and never got uncoiled.............It contained several large streets all very like one another, and many small streets still more like one another, inhabited by people equally like one another, who all went in and out at the same hours, with the same sound upon the same pavements, to do the same work as yesterday and tomorrow, and every year the counterpart of the last and the next.[4]

Having witnessed at first hand the cotton workers strike when travelling north in 1854, the distinguished writer, Charles Dickens here vividly recreated Preston as the fictitious industrial setting of Coketown in his famed novel, *Hard Times*. It was such striking social divisions and continual industrial unrest that led Karl Marx to believe that revolution was in the air as he confidently proclaimed, *Our St. Petersburg is at Preston*! Some seventeen years earlier, on the orders of the first prophet of the Mormon Church, Joseph Smith, American missionaries from the Church of Jesus Christ of Latter Day Saints, having landed in Liverpool, arrived in Preston on 22nd July, just as a general election was taking place. Noticing a banner proclaiming, *Truth Will Prevail*, this they adopted as their motto.

The following day, led by Heber C.K. Kimball, the missionaries attracted a large following to their gathering in Avenham Park. Baptisms took place in the River Ribble as the movement began to establish their first headquarters in Great Britain. One hundred and fifty two years later, the leaders of the Church, based in Utah, proudly announced plans to purchase a fifteen acre site nearby and construct a new northern temple, only the second such building in the British Isles and the fifty second in the world. With its foundation stone laid in June, 1994, and the building completed four years later, the impressive structure, of modern classical design is clad in Sardinian Olympic white granite. It's one hundred and fifty foot tall spire, topped by a golden angel, reigns supreme over the local skyline.

When centuries before, Henry VIII had dissolved the monasteries, the move irrevocably split the county of Lancashire, with the north and east staying true to the Catholic Church, and the south and west taking-up the new Protestant religion. With Catholic emancipation, Preston, very much a bastion of provincial piety, led the way with an ambitious programme of impressive new centres of worship. The Jesuit, St. Ignatius Church on

Meadow Street, was built in 1836 thanks to the £1,300 raised in weekly donations by its parishioners. In nearby Pedder Street, the hugely impressive St Walburge's Church, erected in 1854, and topped by the country's third highest spire, regularly attracted some 6,000 worshippers to Sunday Mass throughout the nineteenth century. Even today, now elevated to city status by Queen Elizabeth II, Preston has the highest percentage of Catholics anywhere in the country.

It was against this ever-changing backdrop that Francis Joseph Thompson was born at 7 Winckley Street, Preston, a somewhat nondescript three storey terraced house, a week before Christmas, on 18th December 1859. His father, Charles Thompson, having qualified in 1847, was a physician specialising in homeopathic medicine. After early appointments in Bristol and Manchester, it was there that he met his wife, Mary Turner Morton. She initially worked in London as a governess. However, following the death of her then fiancée, as a Catholic convert herself, she initially entered the Convent of the Holy Child Jesus, based in St Leonards. Finding it difficult to adjust to the discipline, she moved north to Sale, and was working as a teacher, when she met her future husband.

Following their marriage in 1857, the couple settled in Preston where Dr Thompson set up a practice, initially in St Ignatius Square, at that time on the outskirts of the town and surrounded by numerous fields and meadows. Twelve months prior to the birth of Francis, the couple had lost their first child, Charles Joseph, who lived barely a day. His sister, Mary, was born in 1861, while a second sister, Helen, would die tragically aged only fifteen months. Three years later, another sister, Margaret, completed the family. All were baptized at St Ignatius Church where the family continued to worship, even after moving into the far more elegant surroundings of a nearby Georgian townhouse at 33 Winckley Square. Except for a couple of months at a school run by the Nuns of the Cross and the Passion, the young Francis was looked after at home by a governess and educated by private tutors.

Following two further moves within the same locality, never really seeming at ease in the area, in 1864, when Francis was aged five, the family moved to the small town of Ashton-under-Lyne, some six miles east of Manchester. Once a small hamlet by the side of the River Tame, the discovery of a rich seam of coal during the nineteenth century, quickly quadrupled the population, mostly with an influx of Irish immigrants. It was an area where anti-Catholic sentiment remained strong with William Murphy playing a leading role in a long period of unrest that culminated in serious rioting in the town during Holy Week in 1868. There the Thompson family settled in Stamford Street, at that time far more residential in tone, but now one of the town's major thoroughfares. Initially occupying number 224, on the corner of Brook Street, in 1872, they moved to larger premises at number 226.

St Mary's Roman Catholic Church, situated in nearby Wellington Road, was where Francis Thompson worshipped during the greater part of his life at home. A small Romanesque building with a sharply sloping roof, its once bright red brick, since dulled and worn by the Manchester weather. It was in this church that the poet listened to the sermon on the 3rd Sunday of September, 1885, Our Lady of Sorrows, that would prove to be the inspiration for his poem, *The Passion of Mary*. Returning home, he began work on early drafts of the work that very same evening. Two months later, on the second Sunday in November, Thompson left home, the poem completed while living rough on the streets of London. The sermon at that particular service was preached by the local priest, Canon George Richardson, popularly known throughout the area as The Fighting Canon. His brother subsequently married Thompson's sister, Margaret, and seven years after the poet's mother died, very much to Francis Thompson's utter despair, his father married a second time, the Canon's sister, Annie.

Both by nature and circumstance, the Thompson family appeared to be somewhat isolated, having little general contact with local society. The very few guests to their home tended to be the local priests who were welcomed for a weekly meal after Mass on a Sunday. While remaining distant from his father, who had come to parenthood late in life, Francis particularly doted on his beloved mother. Placing her firmly on a pedestal, she in turn endlessly indulged him. Smothering him in love and rarely able to let him out of her sight, she was seemingly unable to overcome previous family tragedies, having lost both a son and a daughter. In 1867 Francis' maternal grandmother passed away, and later that same year, in December, his mother's father, who lived with the family, died at their home. Each of these deaths had a lasting and devastating effect upon young Francis, then only eight years old.

From an early age, an awed awkward youth, extremely shy and introverted both then and later, he developed a lifelong fascination with military matters. In the company of his sister, alongside endless card games, the pair also each became active devotees of the game of chess. While serving as an altar boy at St Mary's Church, Francis also took part in amateur theatrical productions throughout local parishes. He often seemed more comfortable acting out other people's fantasies than being himself. In looks, rather thin faced with a pale somewhat sallow complexion, his hair dark brown, almost black, only his eyes betrayed a sharpness of intellect. Rarely seen without a book in his hand, he would sit for hours at the bottom of the stairs, devouring the works of Shelley, Macauley, Coleridge and Shakespeare. Much to his mother's annoyance, he would often read aloud:

> When I was a child of seven, standing in my nightgown before the fire, and chatting to my mother, I remember her pulling me up for using a certain word. "That is not used nowadays" she said: "that is one of Shakespeare's words." "It is, Mama?" I said, staring at her disdainfully, "But I did not know that it was one of Shakespeare's words!" "That is just it," she answered, "You have read Shakespeare so much that you are beginning to talk Shakespeare without knowing it. You must take care or people will think you odd.[5]

During his time in Ashton-under-Lyne, Thompson befriended one of his sister's school friends, Lucy Keogh, the daughter of a local judge. She would later find immortality as Lucidè in *Dream Tryst*:

The breaths of kissing night and day
Were mingled in the eastern Heaven:
Throbbing with unheard melody
Shook Lyra all its star-chord seven:
When dusk shrunk cold, and light trod shy,
And dawn's grey eyes were troubled grey;
And souls went palely up the sky,
And mine to Lucidè.

There was no change in her sweet eyes
Since last I saw those sweet eyes shine;
There was no change in her deep heart
Since last that deep heart knocked at mine.
Her eyes were clear, her eyes were Hope's,
Wherein did ever come and go
The sparkle of the fountain-drops
From her sweet soul below.

The chambers in the house of dreams
Are fed with so divine an air,
That Time's hoar wings grow young therin,
And they who walk there are most fair.
I joyed for me, I joyed for her,
Who with the Past meet girt about:
Where our last kiss still warms the air,
Nor can her eyes go out.

Thompson would regularly spend countless hours wandering up and down Church Street in the town, either watching the local clock maker at work or the neighbouring cobbler, Edward Wall, sole and repair shoes. Before he was sent off to board at Stonyhurst College, Thompson's major boyhood friend, Charles Murray, would provide the opposition for Thompson in the endless games of cricket they played at the back of Dunham Terrace. Amid family holidays on the beach, be it at Colwyn Bay in North Wales or Kent's Bank on the North Lancashire coast, brother and sister would happily score Hornby's centuries. Surprisingly, even after leaving Ashton-under-Lyne, Thompson still retained many happy memories of the place. Found among his papers, *To Daisies*, recalls countless halcyon days spent at a noted local beauty spot, Kemp's Fields:

> These hands did toy,
> Children, with you when I was a child,
> And in each other's eyes we smiled:
> Not yours, not yours the grievous-fair
> Apparelling
> With which you wet mine eyes; you wear
> Ah me, the garment of the grace
> I wove you when I was a boy.

It was not only the poet's parents who changed religions but also numerous other family members. Indeed, two of Charles Thompson's sisters, together with a niece entered convent life. The poet's sister, Mary, in 1887, would become Mother Austin of the Presentation Convent in Manchester, while in future years, his sister Margaret's daughter would also become a nun. An uncle, Edward Healy Thompson, once an Anglican clergyman, who later taught English Literature at the Catholic University of Dublin, went on to edit, *The Library of Religious Biography*, a popular series of volumes on the lives of the saints. Yet another uncle, John Costall Thompson, published verse. A particular family friend was a local priest, then the newly-ordained 26 year old Vicar of St Peter's Church in Stalybridge, Canon John Carroll, later to become the Bishop of Shrewsbury. As a former pupil at Ushaw College himself, it was his suggestion that Francis should study there and then undergo training for the priesthood.

Up until that time, Francis Thompson had been idyllically cocooned within the love of a fairly well-to-do professional provincial Catholic family. Doted on by a governess, individual tutors, sisters, parents and close friends, he was happy spending time with his books, his dolls, toy theatre and, not least, his dreams. His first contact with the more brutal aspects of life came in 1870 when, aged eleven, he was sent to the Catholic College of St Cuthbert at Ushaw, some six miles outside Durham. Built to serve the Northern District, its name derives from the ancient Yew Tree that once stood in front of the Junior House. A magnificent symbol of the 19th Century Catholic revival, it had been founded by scholars from the English College at Douai who had fled from France in the aftermath of the French Revolution.

Its austere, yet imposing Gothic appearance, set amid some sixty acres of rolling Durham countryside, is dominated by the grandeur of the Chapel of St. Cuthbert for which the elder Pugin had been the architect. At the other end of the block was the Library for which the Hansom brothers had been responsible. Inside, its fan-vaulting and painted ceiling still bears witness to the best of Victorian Gothic decoration. The Junior College, a self-contained entity throughout Thompson's day was designed by Edward Pugin and had its own much more intimate Chapel of St. Aloysius, together with a refectory, large dormitory and study rooms. Remaining remote from the outside world, each pupil was allocated his own individual patch of garden and expected to take responsibility for its care.

Travelling to the college by train in the company of a senior student, there for the first time, Thompson found boys of his own age often being vindictive and unkind. Among its three hundred pupils were many academically gifted students and Thompson soon found that he could no longer dominate intellectually in quite the same way as he could with his sisters. Somewhat shy, he endured a difficult and challenging first year. While preferring reading to sport, he did however become remarkably proficient in *Cat*, Ushaw's own special game, which while borrowing many qualities from our game of cricket, had originated in Douai. Eventually making his mark both socially and academically, he came top in English, second in Latin and was well above average in all other subjects.

It was while a student at the college that Thompson first began the practice of writing down his thoughts and ideas in an extensive series of notebooks. Even then, they demonstrate a meticulous approach as he constantly drafts and re-drafts his work. While somewhat derivative and heavily influenced by the likes of Shelley, Keats, Coleridge, Wordsworth, Donne and countless others, these early writings show him beginning to appreciate the value of poetry both as a confessional and as a repository of his dreams. Included among the juvenilia is *Lamente Forre Stephanon*, a somewhat pseudo medieval ballad about a sick teacher. It features a number of recurring fingerprints, not least a nostalgia for long vanished childhood pleasures, and the ubiquitous and symbolic sun and moon:

Come listenne to mie roundelaie,
Come droppe he brinie tear with me,
Forre Stephanon is gone awaye,
And long awaye perchance will be!
Our friend hee is sicke,
Gone to take physicke,
Al in the infirmarie.

Swart was hys dresse as the blacke, blacke nyghte,
Whenne the moon dothe not lyghte uppe the waye;
And hys voice was hoarse as the gruffe Northe winde,
Whenne hee swirleth the snowe awaye.
Our friend hee is sicke,
Gone to take physicke,
Al in the infirmarie.

Eyn hee hadde lyke to a hawke,
Soothe I saye, so sharpe was hee,
That hee e'en mought see you talke,
Whenne you talkynge did not bee.
Our friend hee is sicke,
Gone to take physicke,
Al in the infirmarie.

We ne'er schalle see hys lyke agenne,
We ne'er agene hys lyke schalle see,
Searche amonge al Englyshe menne,
You ne'er willfynde the lyke of hee.
Our friend hee is sicke,
Gone to take physicke,
Al in the infirmarie.

Thompson's small circle of school friends tended to centre around those pupils who were somewhat older than himself. Alongside Adam Wilkinson, later a Parish Priest in Newcastle upon Tyne, Thomas Patmore, son of the poet, Coventry Patmore, took particular pride of place. Like Thompson an aspiring poet, he was aged only twenty three when he died in 1883. Nine years older, was another school friend, Paddy Hearn, the Lafcadio Hearn of later life. Born in Greece and abandoned by his mother amid a nomadic lifestyle in Ireland, while at Ushaw, Hearn lost an eye in a playground accident and took a sabbatical for twelve months. After initially forging a literary career in America he then moved to the French West Indies before finally settling in Japan. There, becoming better known as Yakumo Koizumi, he served as Professor of English Literature at the University of Tokyo. He died in 1904.

During his time at Ushaw, Thompson was continually nourished by a Counter Reformation style of Catholicism in which ritual played a major role. Priests and pupils prayed together, and Thompson assisted at Mass and Benediction. Devotion to the Blessed Virgin Mary remained an important element throughout his life and became a recurring theme within his poetry. At times, perhaps, his verses give the impression that external factors such as vestments, lighted tapers, incense and ancient Latin hymns mean far more to him than the religious ideas that lie at the heart of his work. It soon becomes clear that Thompson regards the world as sacramental, and poetry as a form of sanctity.

The central influence in his life at Ushaw was not perhaps to be found in the campus or in the classroom but in the chapel. As a small boy, it was in the Junior Chapel, dedicated to St Aloysius, and later in the main College Chapel that the lay students and clerics prayed together. It seems likely that it was there that Thompson grew immensely in spiritual stature, so much so, that neither the hidden anguish of his subsequent return to Manchester, nor the physical destitution and spiritual desolation of his time spent on the streets of London could ever break him. It is the opinion of Father Terence Connolly[6] that the following lines from Sister Songs may well relate to the years he spent at Ushaw:

From almost earliest youth
I raised the lids o' the truth
And forced her bend on me her shrinking sight;
Ever I knew me Beauty's eremite,
In antre of this lowly body set,
Girt with a thirsty solitude of soul

Everywhere he turned while at college, throughout perhaps his most impressionable years, he was reminded of Our Lady of Ushaw. As you enter the main chapel, hewn in white marble, her statue looks down from the wall of the ante chapel. Throughout the whole month of May, the entire student body and academic faculty would, twice every day, unite in devotions to their Mother and Queen. First came the procession to the altar at the end of the ambulacrum in the seminary, when a motet was performed and prayers said. Later, all would assemble in the ante chapel before a hymn was sung by the entire assembly in unison, each verse then alternating with a choir in harmony, before all joined together for a rousing final verse. The memory of this great festival stayed with Thompson throughout his life.

After spending four years as a junior in the seminary, Thompson entered college for a further course of study. His school record was good: especially in Latin, Greek and English. In 1874, he made the formal decision to move forward to Holy Orders and for the next two years prepared himself for ordination. There seemed to be no obstacle to his advancement and yet, somewhat unexpectedly, his tutors decided that he was unsuited for the priesthood. The chief reason given was: 'a strong nervous timidity and a natural indolence which had always been an obstacle with him'. What his superiors had somewhat perceptively noted, would become a characteristic of his later life; an inability to get out of bed in a morning or apply himself. Deadlines and appointments meant nothing to him.

Early in 1877, his parents back in Ashton-under-Lyne received something of a shock, with the arrival of a warning letter from the College President, Robert Tate;

> I spoke to Frank the other day and he tells me he is quite well and that his own inclinations in regard to the priesthood are not altered, but that his confessor has doubts as to his vocation. He is as he has always been, a very good boy; and I still hope that he will become a good priest. In the meantime, you will not be uneasy about him, as I am sure that his vocation will not be decided precipitately.[7]

Thompson himself, however, was initially reluctant to turn his back on six highly intense years of preparation. Tragically Ushaw's head, Robert Tate, died suddenly that summer. His death was not only a cause of much sorrow for the College, but particularly for Francis Thompson himself. He had long been a particular favourite of Tate's, Thompson's literary outlook seemingly very much in tune with the President's own youthful ambitions. However, by July, the decision had been made. In one of his first acts after acceding to the position of President, Francis Wilkinson, wrote again to the Thompson parents;

> He has always been a remarkably good and obedient boy and certainly one of the cleverest in his class. Still, his nervous timidity has increased to such an extent that I have been most reluctantly compelled to concur in the opinions of his Director and others that it is not the Holy Will of God that he should go on for the Priesthood. It is only after much thought, and after some long and confidential conversations with Frank himself, that I have come to this conclusion: and most unwillingly, for I feel, as I said, a very strong regard and affection for your boy. I earnestly pray God to bless him, and to enable you to bear for His sake the disappointment this has caused……If he can

shake off a natural indolence which has always been an obstacle with him, he has the ability to succeed in any career.[8]

Thompson returned home to his parents in July 1877. Very much a failure in his own eyes and a huge disappointment to his parents, however, he was outwardly welcomed back into the bosom of the family without reproach or recrimination. What now for the failed seminarian? The alternatives would seem to be few. Given his family background, it would have to be either a career in medicine or possibly entry to the legal profession, neither of which he relished. However, with one of England's leading medical schools within easy reach of his home, and his father's many professional contacts, within the month, Thompson had been entered and sat the entrance examination at Owens College in Manchester. Duly accepted, his enrolment took place on 27th September 1877.

All those who knew the young man were utterly shocked by this rather sudden and abrupt change of direction. None more so than a long-time friend and Ashton neighbour, J. Saxon Mills. He was moved to comment, 'an intellectual temperament less adapted to the career of a doctor and a surgeon could not be imagined'.[9] So why did Thompson himself go along with it? Certainly, neither parent ever fully appreciated or remotely seemed to understood their son's literary ambitions. As Thompson later confided to Wilfrid Blunt, 'All my medical studies were wasted, because I would not work, but ran off from my classes to the libraries. If my father had known it, he would not have forced me to go again......I was in every way an unsatisfactory son'.[10]

Founded in 1851 by a bequest of £100,000 from the celebrated Manchester textile merchant, John Owens, Owens College had recently moved from its original Quay Street headquarters to its present home on Oxford Road. In 1880, it went on to become part of Victoria University, before joining with the University of Manchester. Today, a beautiful commemorative tablet, first erected in 1912, thanks to the subscription of friends, family and admirers, proudly records Thompson's connection with the institution. Carved by the renowned sculptor, Eric Gill, the greyish Derbyshire stone makes a highly effective background for the red and black lettering of the inscription:

To the memory of
FRANCIS THOMPSON, POET
1859-1907
STUDENT OF OWENS COLLEGE
1877-1884

What so looks lovelily
Is but the rainbow on life's weeping rain,
Why have longings of immortal pain,
And all we long for mortal? Woe is me,
And all our chants but chaplet some decay.
As mine this vanishing – nay vanished day.

Twelve months after beginning his medical course, Thompson also entered his name in the registers of the Manchester Royal Infirmary. He then divided his time between the College and the hospital. At the heart of his work lay the study of anatomy, requiring him to participate in practical classes in dissection. While initially forcing himself to endure this, increasingly repulsed by the sight of flowing blood, he never ever got used to the many horrors he was forced to witness. Despite his much publicised and somewhat chequered academic record, Thompson's name remains listed as a student in all the University calendars of those years. Somehow, his attendance, or lack of it, never seemed to give anyone in authority any cause for concern.

Caught between his personal involvement with literature and the deeply frustrating demands of a medical course that he increasingly found disagreeable, Thompson escaped the daily tedium of study with numerous alternative pursuits. Tucked away just behind the Infirmary, he spent more and more time in many of Manchester's historic venues, including one of the city's perhaps finest hidden treasures, The Portico Library. Countless days were also spent in the public Central Library, as well as the nearby newly opened Art Gallery in Mosley Street. Spending considerable periods throughout the summer months out of doors, as always, Old Trafford proved a regular and most congenial habitat.

During the holiday periods back in Ashton, when not writing in his room, he would occupy himself with long walks in the neighbouring countryside. He also spent a lot of time with his mother, often going out on trips together. Visits to hear the Hallè Orchestra in Manchester's old Free Trade Hall, did much to raise his spirits. It was his mother also who, in 1879, gave him a copy of Thomas de Quincey's *Confessions of an Opium Eater*. The parallels between the two men are uncanny. Both were writers who enjoyed success as well as notoriety. In childhood, prior to their addiction, both men lived in a dream world. Both left the North West of England for London, were supported by prostitutes, and while initially shaking-off their drug dependency, each invariably returned to it at a later date.

In June 1879, following two years of supposedly highly intensive study, Thompson made his first visit to London to sit the Oxford Local Examinations on behalf of the General Medical Council. In the capital, he stayed in Fulham at 52 Tregunter Road with a cousin, William Costall May. After the examination, having enjoyed a visit to the opera, he then spent a most fascinating time at the South Kensington Museum (now the Victoria and Albert Museum). There he viewed an impressive exhibition of artefacts from Troy, loaned to the museum by the German archaeologist, Heinrich Schliemann. Not able to forget seeing a cup on display which was identified as the Amphicypellon of Homer, it subsequently provided him with the first title of one of his longest ever poems.

Back home in Ashton, a few days later, reality again intruded as the results came through; he had failed. Returning to Owens College, Thompson made a further attempt to apply himself. If he was not yet a confirmed addict, he was certainly, by now dabbling extensively in all manner of drugs. One of his most common mixtures, much favoured by the cotton spinners, was a tincture of laudanum, a drink made from opium and mixed with alcohol or distilled water. Camphorated tincture of opium, or paregoric was also widely available and in Britain there were countless patent medicines such as Godfrey's Cordial, Dover's Powder or Mrs Winslow's Soothing Syrup.

These were the first over the counter, self-administered drugs. Companies were not obliged to list the ingredients and their products proved highly popular. In London, De Quincey wrote that 'the number of amateur opium eaters was immense'. No less so in Manchester where opium was cheap and plentiful. On Saturday afternoons, the counters of the chemists would be strewn with grains of the drug ready for the evening demand. Mothers used it to keep babies quiet while, for the workers, it helped them to sleep at night. Opiates had provided De Quincey's generation with a means of escaping the ravages of the mechanical age. For the more intellectual, it supposedly stimulated creativity.

Not long after Thompson's return home from London, his mother developed a serious liver complaint. Increasingly infirm, she would die barely six months later, on the 19th December 1879, just a day after her beloved son's twentieth birthday. Aged only 58, the death certificate simply records; Hypertrophy of liver six months. She was interred close by in Dukinfield Cemetery, a short walk from the Thompson family home. Possibly his last chance of a normal life was buried with her, for while his father treated his son with continual generosity, he never fully seemed to quite understood the boy's literary leanings. His sister always fervently believed that had his mother been alive, Thompson would never have left home.[11]

The only echo of this sad event was an unpublished poem that appeared many years later. It affords a painfully vivid insight into the soul of this greatly troubled young man;

Son of the womb of her,
Loved till doom of her,
Thought of the brain of her,
Heart of her side:
She joyed and grieved in him,
Hoped, believed in him:
God grew fain of her,
And she died.

Died; and horribly
Saw the mystery,
Saw the grime of it-
That hid soul;
Saw the sear of it,
Saw the fear of it,
Saw the slime of it;
Saw it whole!
O mother! Mother! For all the sweet John saith,
O mother was not *this* the Second Death?

Following his mother's death, Francis was initially cared for by his sister, Mary. Such was his thin and emaciated figure, that he was dubbed locally as "Elasticlegs." A fellow student, Robert MacKenna later recalled in a volume entitled, *As Shadows Lengthen*, 'that he was loose-limbed, with a vacant stare, weak lips and a usually half-open mouth, the saliva often trickling over his chin. He was the butt and jest of the many school boys who used to travel by the same train and who tormented him unmercifully'.[12] On three occasions Thompson failed his medical examinations, first in 1879, and the second in 1881. The last attempt was sat in Glasgow instead of London in 1884. His father fervently hoped that the Scottish examiners would be more lenient. Sadly it proved rather a forlorn hope.

In the interim, Thompson had taken a break from his studies. Overcome by illness, it seems in all probability that he had suffered a serious mental breakdown. By now, he was being cared for by his sisters. After being forced to leave college, he had a spell of some sixteen months experiencing a varied range of employment opportunities. Most surprisingly, given his recent history, he was initially apprenticed to a Manchester surgical instrument maker. This ended after just two weeks. He then became an encyclopaedia salesman, but instead of trying to sell the volumes, he just sat down and read them. Eventually he enlisted in the army, again serving for only a few weeks before yet a further rejection. Supposedly this was because his chest did not measure up to the size required!

His many sufferings, both physical and mental, were to a large extent, self-induced. His often inconsiderate self-centred behaviour, invariably alienated not only his parents, but also many of those who tried to help, as Thompson continually sought to escape the responsibilities of adult life. And yet his notebooks from this time reveal a constant struggle to conform and follow a pattern which he knew his church demanded. To the few allowed access to his inner self, he was much admired for his intelligence and rare spiritual insight. Indeed, at a deeper emotional and spiritual level, he constantly displayed great mental toughness. While his pain found a ready outlet in his poetry, this was invariably compounded by the constant stream of rejection slips he invariably received from publishers.

By now, external events were very quickly spiralling out of Francis Thompson's immediate control. With his younger sister, Margaret, engaged to be married, she would soon depart to live in Canada, never to return. His other sister, Mary, would also soon move away to become a nun in an enclosed order, based behind high walls, in Livesey Street in Manchester. There, any contact, even with close family, was forbidden. It was on the Feast of the Presentation, 2nd February, 1887, that she became a Novice of the Congregation of the Presentation, an order originally founded in Ireland by Nano O'Nagle. Two years later, on the Feast of the Exaltation of the Holy Cross, she took her vows becoming Mother Austin. She would remain contentedly in the Convent for the next fifty seven years.[13]

The final straw for Thompson came with his father's impending second marriage to Annie Richardson, the sister of the local clergyman. She had little time for Francis and made her feelings plain. It seems she had become aware, as had the majority of the family, of his drug addiction. She considered him very much a ne'er-do-well who, at the age of 26, had failed at everything his family had planned for him. The final denouement came when his father, increasingly prompted by his wife, confronted his son and accused him of having a drink problem. Francis vehemently denied this, but later on that fateful day, Sunday 8th November 1885, having left a note in his sister Margaret's room, he stole unnoticed from the house and set off on foot to walk the seven or so miles to Manchester. From there, having written home to request some money for the fare, he lingered for a week, living on the proceeds of the sale of his possessions. He then set off to travel to London.

Having, unbeknown to his father, gone through a long period of despondency, particularly following the death of his beloved mother, Thompson abruptly cut all ties with his family, moved away, to begin a new life never to return. Quite what his plan was seems unclear. He just had to get away.

> I made the journey to the capital without hope, and with the gloomiest of forebodings, very much in the desperate spirit of an *enfant perdu*.[14]

Dr Charles Thompson

Mary Thompson

Francis Thompson with his sisters

Thompson's step mother Annie

Preston Marketplace, 1859

7 Winckley Street

Stamford Street, Ashton-under-Lyne

Francis Thompson, aged 15

Lafcadio Hearn

Ushaw College

MANCHESTER ROYAL INFIRMARY.

SESSION 1878 to 1879

We, the undersigned, promise to observe and obey the Bye-Laws and Regulations which may from time to time be passed by the General Board and Medical Staff of the Manchester Royal Infirmary, in reference to the attendance of Students upon the practice of the Hospital; and consent to submit to our Certificates being withheld, or such other penalties as may be determined upon, in case of non-compliance with the aforesaid Rules and Regulations.

Name.	Postal Address.
Francis Joseph Thompson	226 Stamford Street, Ashton-Under-Lyne
Alfred Taylor	Crompton Fold, Breightmet, Nr Bolton
Clement Bernard Voisey	Park Leigh, Alexandra Rd Manchester
John Metcalfe Beverley	37 Derbys, Manchester Rd Bury.

Admission Register, Manchester Royal Infirmary

Francis Thompson

Illustrations by Gustave Doré from the book, London, published 1872

Left: Opium Smoking
Bottom Left: The Bull's-Eye
Bottom Right: Under the Arches

Alice and Wilfrid Meynell

Chapter 2

PITCHED BETWIXT HEAVEN AND CHARING CROSS

> With little more luggage than a few extra pieces of clothing and with Blake and Aeschylus stuffed in his pockets, Thompson arrived in London in December 1885. He was nearly twenty-six years old and carried the marks of the provinces on him in his Lancashire accent which Viola Meynell calls *slight* but W.S. Blunt *broad*. He was thin, with ill-covered shoulder blades, although he carried himself bravely upright, a large self-indulgent mouth, not yet veiled with the straggly moustache and beard of later years, and large, melancholy eyes. Although he did not know it, he was to become spiritually one of a band of literary men, the beat generation of the late eighties and nineties, including Lionel Johnson, Ernest Dowson, Aubrey Beardsley, who were pursuing the decadent muse through the sinuous corridors of disordered lives.[1]

The celebrated New Zealand university lecturer and Catholic writer, John Cowie Reid here eloquently setting the scene for what would become the next important chapter in the increasingly chaotic life of Francis Thompson. The passage above first appeared in the course of his important autobiography of the writer entitled, *Francis Thompson: Man and Poet* and published in this country by Routledge and Kegan Paul in 1959.

One of Thompson's first acts following his arrival in the capital was to inform his sister, Mary, of the address of the reading room in the Strand where she was to send his agreed weekly allowance of seven shillings. After a little while, he failed to collect the money and the allowance subsequently ceased to be sent. In the meantime, Thompson had quickly found work as a collector for one of the city's more than two hundred book stores, based in Panton Street. His role was to gather together a sack full of volumes for his employer from the wholesalers. Typically, the job lasted only a matter of weeks, as once again, Thompson spent more time reading the books rather than delivering them.

With laudanum increasingly taking priority over food and lodging, Thompson proved remarkably adept at learning the economics of the poor, particularly where to buy the cheapest food. During the day he initially found refuge for a time in the free Library at the historic Guildhall. However, increasingly unkempt and unwashed, his way was eventually barred by a then young assistant librarian, Bernard Kettle:

> It fell to my lot to have to perform the painful duty of asking him to forgo his visits here. He always came in with two books in his pocket. One, I think, was Sophocles; and had I known that I was entertaining an "angel unawares" I should perhaps have been more reluctant to eject him.[2]

He also spent much time in the National Gallery. One painting in particular, Rossetti's *Interpretation of the Annunciation, Ecce Ancilla Domine*, now housed in the Tate Gallery, inspired an early poem of quite striking promise. Here Thompson recreates Rossetti's visual imagery, displaying an increasingly mature and distinctive voice:

> This angel's feet, winged with aspiring light,
> That kindles its own image in the floor;
> His gravely noble face, serene in might
> From gazing on the Godhead evermore;
> This lily shining from the lilied land,
> Making a breath of heaven in the room;
> Yon Dove, whose presence tells how near at hand
> The mystical conception of her womb:
> Were *these* the things that roused from holy dreams
> To holier waking the elected maid?
> Absorbed in all the great to-be she seems,
> With pensive eyes that yet are not afraid.
> Soon her low voice shall ratify heaven's will,
> And hell's gate groan, and death's stern heart stand still.

Among the other numerous scribbled fragments that constantly adorned his early note books is, *The Owl*. A bird traditionally the messenger of death, it is yet another poem deeply coloured by Thompson's all-encompassing drug dependency:

The owl has eyes that bicker and gleam,
And a hooked foul nose as may well beseem;
And she laughs out loud with a whooping note,
She laughs out bale from her rusty throat;
Why does she laugh from her rusty throat?
She laugheth at sleep that sleepeth not.

The owl is the witch of the cauldron of sleep:
And she stirs it and seeths it whooping deep;
And she thrusts the witch-bits into it deep,
Gendering ghosts for the smoke of sleep.
She flings in toads from the money-dust,
And feeds it thick with the dead fat of lust;
Corpse-limbs of love, yet quivering new;
And blood of the thoughts that are writhing too,
Drawn from the place where the pang went through:
Adders of longing and fanged regrets;
Winged lizards of terror and monstrous threats!
Ah, horrible terrors, the withering threats!
And she sees with her eyes which the fires look through
Her deep sleep-cauldron, reeking new;
And she laughs at sleep, tu-whit, tu-whoo!

And so murk is the sleep smoke of despair,
And so awful the spectres rising there,
And so fearful they throng on the calm night air,
That were not sleep as brief as deep,
It were better almost to die than sleep!

For a brief period until moved on by the local constabulary at the request of concerned shop keepers, Francis Thompson managed to earn a somewhat slender living occupying a pitch as a boot black. Other methods of obtaining a few pence for his daily subsistence included the hawking of newspapers and matches, assisting in the unloading of baggage at hotels, calling cabs for theatre goers and holding the reins of carriage horses. With often little money for a bed, even in the worst of the capital's numerous doss houses, he would spend the night somewhere on the streets. Surprisingly, as he wandered alone in the Strand, though he had relatives living close by within easy reach in Church Court, he never attempted contact.

In an essay reviewing General Booth's 1890 volume on the Salvation Army, *In Darkest England*, Thompson, using the nom de plume, Francis Tancred, offers an eloquent glimpse of what life was like for him:

> I have knowledge, not indeed great or wide, but within certain narrow limits more intimate than most men's, of this life, our common sleep, precious, costly and fallible, as water in a wilderness; in which men rob and women vend themselves – for fourpence.[3]

He goes on to describe the conditions he encountered at the Southampton Row shelter:

> What such an institution does, and how much remains to do, may be impressively realised by one who watches the nightly crowd of haggard men outside this refuge; the anxious waiting while the ticket holders are slowly admitted, the thrill-the almost shudder-through the crowd when the manager emerges to pick out men for the vacant beds left over after the ticket holders' admission, the sickening suspense and fear in all eyes as-choosing a man here and there-he passes along the huddled ranks, the cold clang with which the gates of mercy in those fortunate few, but out the rest; and then the hopeless, helpless drifting off the dreary crowd.[4]

As he faced his second winter on the streets, still living rough, Thompson was then rescued by a kindly bootmaker, John McMaster, owner of a successful business, based at 14 Panton Street, just off Leicester Square. The pair met one day in Wardour Street when something about Thompson first attracted McMaster's attention. A devout Anglican of evangelical outlook and a Church Warden at St Martin-in-the-Fields, McMaster had long sought out young men who might benefit from regular employment. Found lodgings close to the shop and given a job as a messenger, Thompson was even trusted to look after the McMaster's young children. Given a boy's work to do and a wage of five shillings a week, he was more a guest than an employee.

After Thompson had told McMaster about his Lancashire background McMaster, having checked the facts, then invited Dr Thompson to London in order to attempt something of a family reconciliation. As a result, in December 1886, a neatly attired Thompson, briefly free of drugs, paid a fortnight's visit back to Ashton-under-Lyne to spend the Christmas break with his family. However, with his sister now in the throes of entering a convent and his father's second marriage to Annie Richardson imminent, any hope of a lasting reconciliation proved entirely problematical. On his way back to London, Thompson stopped-off to spend some time in Manchester and resume his drug habit.

Sadly, within weeks of returning to his job in London, Thompson's increased indolence forced McMaster to sack him. Parting company in the middle of January 1887, McMaster later spoke of Thompson as his only failure. As he related in the 1916 volume he compiled on the history of St Martin-in-the-Fields, he had no idea of Thompson's later fame until many years after the poet's death. In the interim, Thompson had delighted in discussing literary and religious matters with the boot maker's father. From such discussions began to develop the seed of an important essay that would come to change the poet's life, *Paganism Old and New*.

The poet's father, Dr Thompson married for a second time, Annie Richardson, in Ashton-under-Lyne on 27 April, 1887. His son did not attend the ceremony, though it seems the newly-weds did subsequently travel to London to try and find him. By now having left McMaster's employment, Thompson was back again living rough. His second sister, Margaret, who initially emigrated to Canada, later moved to live permanently in Los Angeles. In 1891, shortly before his death, Dr Thompson changed his will to give precedence to the newly-born son of his second marriage, Norbert Thompson. Out of an estate valued at £1,500, he left Margaret £100, but nothing at all to his first-born son. Francis was still being labelled by the family as "a failure and rather a disgrace."[5]

At the time, 28 years old and with a legacy of sorrow left behind in his native Lancashire, a handful of verses was all Thompson had to show for his talents as an aspiring writer. Attempting to sell some of his early work to several journals, invariably the response was rejection after rejection. As Thompson sank lower and lower into destitution, for a brief period, as he later somewhat starkly related, suicide seemed to be his only way out. He was saved, he always claimed, by a vision of the eighteenth century English poet, Thomas Chatterton, whose own precocious talents were cruelly ended by his own hand:

> It was in an empty space behind Covent Garden Market where the gardeners throw their rubbish that, just before, I had resolved on suicide. I then spent all my remaining pence on laudanum, one large dose, and I went there to take it. I had swallowed half when I felt an arm laid across my chest, and looking up saw Thomas Chatterton standing over me and forbidding me to drink the other half. Having recognised him from his portrait, I remembered at once the story of the money which arrived for him the day after his suicide.[6]

However, as he now approached his third winter, still destitute and homeless, help came in the unlikely form of one of the many hundreds of prostitutes who regularly worked the area around Soho and the Strand. While her name is not known, nor any details of their first meeting, we do know that a regular and warm relationship between the couple subsequently developed. When her assignations were over, she would take him back to her lodgings in Brompton. With her he seems to have found a rare and stimulating companionship that, at that particular time, served him well. This somewhat unusual relationship has long remained a constant source of fascination for future writers and dramatists.

Later, suddenly disappearing after feeling that her usefulness was at an end, Thompson's often frenzied attempts to trace her inexorably implicated him as a suspect in the notorious Whitechapel murders, when five prostitutes died at the hands of the infamous Jack the Ripper. Highly pertinent in the context of the case remains Thompson's undeniable professional anatomical expertise and knowledge. This came to the fore through his somewhat disturbingly graphic poetry of the time, particularly, *Ballad of the Witch Babies*, which tells of a lusty knight who roams the darkness hunting down and disembowelling young women.

Perhaps not a moment too soon, salvation came in the unlikely form of magazine editor, Wilfrid Meynell and his wife, Alice. While his family had washed their hands of him, his old friend, Canon John Carroll, had not. He continued to urge the poet to send some of his writings to a Catholic literary journal, *Merry England*. Thus, towards the end of February 1887, using for postage his last halfpenny, Thompson had placed an article and some poetry in an envelope and sent them to the magazine's offices at 43 Essex Street. Little could he have foreseen the outcome of his actions.

February 23/87

Dear Sir

In enclosing the accompanying article for your inspection, I must ask pardon for the soiled state of the manuscript. It is due, not to slovenliness but to the strange places and circumstances under which it has been written. For me, no less than Parolles, the dirty nurse experience has something fouled. I enclose a stamped envelope for a reply; since I do not desire the return of the manuscript, regarding your judgement of its worthlessness as quite final. I can hardly expect that where my prose fails my verse will succeed. Nevertheless, on the principle of "will I try the last," I have added a few specimens of it, with the off-chance that one may be less poor than the rest. Apologizing very sincerely for my intrusion on your valuable time, I remain

Yours with little hope
Francis Thompson

Kindly address your rejection to The Charing Cross Post Office. *The Editor of Merry England*

Seven years older than Francis Thompson, Wilfrid John Meynell, the seventh of eight children, was born at Picton House, Newcastle-on-Tyne in November 1852. Both his father, the owner of a local coal mine, and his mother, a member of the illustrious Tuke family who famously collaborated with William Wilberforce in the fight against slavery, were long-standing Quakers. Meynell was educated initially at Bootham School, York, before moving to board at Ackworth School, near Pontefract in West Yorkshire. His illustrious great grandfather's great-great-grandfather, William Tuke had, in 1660, been imprisoned in York as a conscientious objector. However, at the age of eighteen, Wilfrid Meynell had left the Society of Friends to become a Roman Catholic. Daughter Viola later wrote:

> As a Catholic he had never quite shed his Quakerism. He had a Quaker's flair for business and a Quaker's industry; was for lost causes, lame dogs and forlorn friends, and for individual interpretation of dogmas, and generous adjustments of errancies in others. He bought with him into Catholicism his Quaker experiences of a strong sense of the reality and presence of God. The Church that he joined was for him the Church of the Scriptures, and he was apt to see all problems in scriptural terms; mysteries of religion did not arise.[7]

Subsequently moving to London, Meynell lodged with Father William Lockhart at the priest's house at St Ethelreda's Church in Ely Place, Holborn. Originally a monastic chapel purchased by Father Lockhart in 1873 for the Rosminians, who were also known as the Fathers of Charity, the first Mass being celebrated at the church the following year. Previously Lockhart had been a close friend and disciple of Cardinal Newman. At St Ethelreda's he had thrown open the doors of the presbytery to young men attempting to make their way in the capital. While lodging there, alongside parish duties, Meynell was beginning his foray into Catholic journalism. Soon flourishing, he would go on to succeed Cardinal Manning as Editor of the Catholic newspaper, *The Weekly Register*.

In 1876, when aged 24, Meynell had become totally entranced by a sonnet, quoted in a review of *Preludes*, a first volume of poetry from the pen of the poet, Alice Thompson. No relation to Francis Thompson, Alice Christine Gertrude Thompson was born at Barnes in Surrey on 11th October 1847, the younger daughter of Thomas James Thompson, a long-standing friend of Charles Dickens, and his wife, Christine Weller. Both Alice and her elder sister, Elizabeth, spent much of their early years travelling extensively throughout Europe. Both the Thompson girls were educated privately, before Elizabeth became a student at the Female School of Art in South Kensington, later to become a highly distinguished painter, particularly noted for her battle scenes.

The family later settled for a time in Malvern where Alice, now aged twenty, was received into the Catholic Church. Unfortunately, while undertaking instruction, a passionate love affair developed between her and her instructor, the local parish priest, thirty five year old Father Augustus Dignam. As a result, the priest was summarily sent abroad to work. He would not be the last to be captivated by her charm. Alice's sorrow eventually found its way into much of her early work, most notably *Renouncement* and *Letter From A Girl To Her Own Old Age*. In a short space of time she would soon develop into one of the most sought after literary personalities of the age.

Having used his rapidly increasing and ever-spreading influential coterie of social contacts, Meynell was able to eventually engineer a meeting with Alice. Again, like so many others, he too was totally captivated by her charm and personality. Surprisingly, there was strong initial parental opposition to their union. Despite this, their romance quickly blossomed. Becoming engaged on New Year's Day, 1877, in a matter of months, the couple were married by the Bishop of Nottingham at the Church of the Servite Fathers on 16th April 1877. Elder sister Elizabeth, soon followed suit, marrying the distinguished Irish Catholic soldier, Major William Butler, a mere three months later.

Together with the obligatory domestic servant, Wilfrid and Alice began their married life at 11 Inkerman Terrace, Kensington, living next to Alice's parents. It was there that five of their surviving seven children - Sebastian, Monica, Everard, Madeline, Viola and Vivian, who died in early infancy, were born. Amid a somewhat haphazard household, it was E.V. Lucas who once most perceptively wrote of Alice as, "A priestess set in the midst of children, sharing their nonsense but thinking her own thoughts."[8] When Coventry Patmore later fell hopelessly in love with her, feeling threatened, she severed all connection with him. She would later do the same with fellow writer, George Meredith.

Working from home, in 1880, the couple embarked on their first venture together, *The Pen, A Literary Journal*, which sadly closed after a mere seven editions. Twelve months later, at the request of old friend, Cardinal Manning and engaged at a salary of £300 per year, Meynell took over the editorship of *The Weekly Register*. Priced at threepence, post free, and published at 3 p.m. every Friday, its thirty two pages were devoted to church reports, diocesan and parochial events. Designed as a rival to the much more conservative

Tablet, for *The Weekly Register*, Alice contributed leaders, reviewed books, read proofs and translated Papal encyclicals.

In 1881 the couple, now both very much in demand, moved to a larger home in Phillimore Place, adding a further servant to the household. A bequest from Alice's late father then allowed them to buy a spacious plot of land and subsequently build a striking new house in Palace Court, then a quiet cul-de-sac in Bayswater. This most impressive of buildings, designed by the distinguished architect, Leonard Stokes, and costing £1,500, comprised a dining room and morning room on the ground floor, drawing room and a library on the next with ten bedrooms and dressing rooms above. With Kensington Gardens as their playground, it was at Palace Court, that Olivia and Francis duly arrived to complete the ever expanding Meynell family.

In addition to writing, reviewing and editing two newspapers of their own, Alice and Wilfrid were soon among the busiest journalists in London. While their rapidly growing family brood enjoyed something of an idyllic childhood, they could not fail to notice that they were the recipients of a warm, yet invariably preoccupied affection. "Blandishments we had little of," daughter Viola once reportedly said. She went on, "We were taken to our mother's arms but briefly: exquisitely fondled but with economy, as if there were work always to be resumed. We were at once the most befriended of children, yet the most slighted."

While at the helm of *The Weekly Register* for eighteen years, in 1883, Meynell launched a new monthly illustrated magazine, which he entitled, *Merry England*. Jointly owned initially with Messrs Burns and Oates, after a mere twelve months, Meynell became the sole proprietor. Providing a mouthpiece for liberal ideas, it was the first serious attempt at spreading an intelligent appreciation of English literature among English Catholics. At its core lay the ideas of William Morris in tandem with the aims of the Young England Movement. A portrait of Benjamin Disraeli, Lord Beaconsfield, proudly adorned the front cover of its first edition. Its title was taken by Meynell from Wordsworth's sonnet;

> They called the Merry England in old time;
> A happy people won for thee that name,
> With envy heard in many a distant clime;
> And, spite of change, for me thou keepst the same
> Endcaring title, a responsive chime
> To the heart's strong belief. . .
> . . .Can, I ask,
> This face of rural beauty be a mask
> For discontent, and poverty, and crime?

These spreading towns a cloak for lawless will?
Forbid it, Heaven! – that Merry England still
May be thy rightful name, in prose and rhyme.

Very much at the vanguard of progressive Catholicism, the publication was never slow to embrace non-Catholic ideas and interests. Indeed, neither were contributors confined solely to Catholics, as among its writers were W.H. Hudson, J.L. Garvin, St John Adcock, Hilaire Belloc and Lionel Johnson. The numerous reviews of books increasingly became a means of writing extended essays on the subjects at hand. In addition to literary themes, articles regularly focussed on local history and architecture. Even Cardinal Manning himself would not be slow to contribute and comment on any topical religious or ethical matters of concern.

This work-a-day newspaper for the laity, published from offices above a bookshop at 43 Essex Street, immediately proved popular, its initial print run of 5,000 copies selling out. Most of its content emanated from both Wilfrid and Alice. Here they regularly appeared in many and various guises. Among the numerous pseudonyms used was John Oldcastle. Some years earlier, John Oldcastle had also been the author of the popular primer, *Journals and Journalism*. Another regular contributor was named as Francis Phillimore. Other articles were merely signed A.C. Opie, meaning a copy.

Constantly under pressure to meet weekly deadlines, Wilfrid Meynell was invariably somewhat lax in dealing with day-to-day matters that involved correspondence. Thompson's manuscripts, most uninviting in outward aspect were pigeon-holed, unread by a much occupied editor. Therefore, it would be almost twelve months or more before Meynell, in a rare bout of housekeeping, got around to opening Thompson's long-neglected parcel. Upon eventually examining its scruffy and almost illegible contents, he was both surprised and taken aback with what he found. His wife too, was no less impressed. He then immediately sent a letter to the address at the head of the note, Charing Cross Post Office. After some weeks it found its way back to Meynell, returned unopened.

In the interim, an increasingly intrigued Wilfrid Meynell began to make enquires of his own about his mysterious contributor, Francis Thompson. However, despite his best endeavours, all his efforts repeatedly came to naught. In the end, he decided to try to draw the author out by publishing in the April edition of *Merry England*, *The Passion of Mary*. This Crashaw-like quatrain on the sorrows of the Virgin had, a couple of years earlier, begun life at the family's Ashton-under-Lyne dining table. Here its closing reminder of Thompson's years spent on the streets gives the work a particular poignancy:

O Thou who dwellest in the day!
Behold I pace amidst the gloom:
Darkness is ever round my way
With little space for sunbeam-room.

Yet Christian sadness is divine
Even as *thy* patient sadness was:
The salt tears in our life's dark wine
Fell in it from the saving cross.

Bitter the bread of our repast;
Yet doth a sweet the bitter leaven:
Our sorrow is the shadow cast
Around it by the light of Heaven.

O light in Light, shine down from Heaven!

On receiving his copy of the April edition, a surprised and delighted Canon John Carroll, immediately alerted the author, imploring him to visit the *Merry England* office and make contact with the editor. Thus, on the 14th April 1888, Francis Thompson wrote yet again to Wilfrid Meynell;

Dear Sir

In the last days of February or the first days of March, 1887, (my memory fails me as to the exact date) I forwarded to you for your magazine a prose article, ("Paganism Old and New," or "Ancient and Modern," for I forget which wording I adopted) and accompanied it by some pieces of verse, on the chance that if the prose failed, some of the verse might meet acceptance. I enclosed a stamped envelope for reply, since (as I said) I did not desire the return of the manuscript. Imprudently perhaps, instead of forwarding the parcel through the post, I dropped it with my own hand into the letter-box of 43 Essex Street. There was consequently no stamp on it, since I did not think a stamp would be necessary under the circumstances. I asked you to address your answer to the Charing Cross Post Office.

To be brief, from that day to this, no answer has ever come into my hands. And yet, more than a twelve-month since the forwarding of the manuscript, I am now informed that one of the copies of the verse I submitted to you (i.e. "The Passion of Mary") is appearing in this month's issue of "Merry England." Such an occurrence I can only explain to myself in one way; viz. that some untoward accident cut off your means of communicating with me.

To suppose otherwise,-to suppose it intentional-would be to wrong your known honour and courtesy. I have no doubt that your explanation, when I receive it, will be entirely satisfactory to me. I therefore enclose a stamped and addressed envelope for an answer, hoping that you will recompense me for my long delay by the favour of an early reply. In any case, however long circumstance may possibly delay your reply, it will be sure of reaching me at the address I have now given.

I remain
Yours respectfully
Francis Joseph Thompson

P.S. Doubtless, when I received no answer, I ought to have written again. My excuse must be that a flood-tide of misfortune rolled over me, leaving me no leisure to occupy myself with what I regarded as an attempt that had hopelessly failed. Hence my entire subsequent silence.

The letterhead bore the name of a chemist's shop in Drury Lane, a mere short walk from the *Merry England* offices. Eventually deciding to visit the premises himself, on arrival Meynell was presented with an unpaid bill for Thompson's laudanum of three and ninepence. Happy to settle the bill, increasingly desperate, he then promised further money to the shopkeeper if he would persuade Thompson to visit his nearby headquarters. As the weeks passed, a despairing Meynell was just about to give up on his quest, when midway through May, a dishevelled twenty nine year old derelict in a shabby brown overcoat and even shabbier boots, eventually appeared at his door. Meynell later recalled the event in conversation with fellow writer, Wilfrid Blunt:

When he came into the room, he half opened the door and then retreated and did so twice before he got courage to come inside. He was in rags, his feet, without stockings, showing through his boots, his coat torn, and no shirt. He seemed in the last stages of physical collapse. I asked him how being in such a condition, he had been able to consult the books out of which he had gathered the quotations for his essay. He answered: "Books I have none, but Blake and the Bible." All the quotations had been made from memory.[9]

Despite Thompson's extremely gaunt and neglected appearance, he was still able to retain a distinction which a non-judgemental Wilfrid Meynell found not only fascinating but also hugely impressive. Throughout their short meeting, Thompson maintained a certain reserve, initially refusing the offer of a weekly sum of money for food and lodging. While talking much of his books, he revealed little of his own personal circumstances. However, much to Meynell's relief, he did eventually agree to the publication of his essay, *Paganism Old and New* in the forthcoming June edition of *Merry England.* He also promised to return in a matter of days so that they could check the proofs together.

A few weeks later, invited to Phillimore Place to dine with the Meynell family, it was there that Thompson met, for the first time, Alice Meynell. It was a true turning point in Thompson's career and for the rest of his all-too short life, he became a permanent and regular welcome visitor to the household. It soon became his true parental home. Though close to the whole family, who provided him with shelter, both physically and emotionally, it was Alice who became his muse, his protectress, and the inspirer of much of his poetry. Happily, his romantic unpurposive love for her offered no bar to happy relationships with all the family, be they young or old. If he had a home at all it would be with those who now protected him and assured him of the worth of everything that he valued most.

If Alice was his lost mother and Wilfrid his lost father, by now, having won his trust, he was soon becoming amenable to the Meynell's many offers of help. One result being that Thompson allowed himself to undergo a detailed examination by a doctor. As an immediate consequence, he was deemed to be in urgent and serious need of hospital treatment. Agreeing to undergo such a spell, Thompson then spent six weeks in an isolation ward. While there, starved of the drug he once so steadfastly craved, he wrote *Not Even In Dreams*, a work that offers a direct reference to his problems:

This love is crueller than the other love:
    We had the Dreams for Tryst, we other pair;
But here there is no we; not anywhere
    Returning breaths of sighs about me move.
No wings, even of the stuff which fancy move,
    Perturb Sleep's air with responsive flight
When mine sweeps into dreams. My soul in fright
    Circles as round its widowed nest the dove.

One shadow but usurps another's place:
    And, though this shadow more enthralling is,
Alas, it has no lips at all to miss!
    I have not even that former poignant bliss,
That haunting sweetness, that forlorn sad trace,
    The phantom memory of a vanished kiss.

Another poem from the same period, *Non Pax-Expectatio*, reveals further the torments and challenges, as Thompson underwent what amounted to a demanding period of substance withdrawal. Today we would perhaps categorise this as going 'cold turkey'. The poem's title, somewhat strangely prophetic in the circumstances, is perhaps more readily paraphrased than translated: *Not permanent peace, but a respite with expectancy of a struggle soon to be renewed.*

> Hush! 'tis the gap between two lightnings. Room
> Is none for peace in this thou callest piece,
> This breathing-while wherein the breathings cease.
> The pulses sicken, hearkening through the gloom.
> Afar the thunders of a coming doom
> Ramp on the cowering winds. Lo! At the dread,
> Thy heart's tomb yawns and renders up its dead-
> The hopes 'gainst hope embalmèd in the womb.

By December 1888, now out of hospital and living in new lodgings in Paddington, the Meynell family visited him daily. Beginning to write once more, particularly prose, a book review quickly grew into a major article on John Bunyan's *Pilgrim's Progress*. This would take the lead position in the November edition of *Merry England*. He also began writing for *The Dublin Review*. However, while extremely concerned about the poet's more immediate short-term health issues, the family were also keen to help turn his long-dormant literary ambitions into future productive reality. Becoming the subject of much thought, discussion and debate, the Meynell's then made Francis Thompson a somewhat surprising offer and one, which in the circumstances, he felt he simply could not afford to turn down.

Chapter 3

STORRINGTON AND PANTASAPH

Saved from the imminent death once so confidently prophesied by more than one eminent member of the medical profession, it was thanks to Meynell's munificence, that the next stop on Francis Thompson's remarkable journey took him to Storrington in West Sussex. One of the oldest settlements in the country, first mentioned in the Domesday Book, it is one of a series of villages that straddle the ancient trackway from Ditchling Beacons to Lewes. Adding to its overall historic ambience remains its historic parish church, which bears traces dating back to both Norman and Saxon times. In the sixteenth century the Rector bequeathed an area of land, known as Curfew Acre, for which the rent was designated for the nightly tolling of the church's great bell.

It was to this rural outpost in 1881, a mere eight years before Thompson arrived, that a small group of monks, fleeing from religious persecution in France, chose to put down roots. The Canons of Prémontré, their monastery becoming known as the Priory of Our Lady of England, settled near Kithurst Hill, occupying land generously bequeathed to them by the Duke of Norfolk. Sent to the locality in February 1889, Thompson remained amid the community for twelve months, moving back to London in February, 1890. Meynell had two motives in sending him there: one was to improve his health away from the capital's polluted air; the other was to make sure that he was cut off completely from any access to opium.

Having by now reached the age of 30, Thompson still had only two rather ordinary poems to his name. However, while still struggling to overcome his drug addiction, he soon found his new surroundings increasingly stimulating. Amid his enforced abstinence and despite the constant anguish of his withdrawal symptoms, suddenly poetry began to spill out of him in a remorseless torrent. But before then, Thompson had to attend to more practical matters:

> I am, as I expected to be, very ill just now; so that you must excuse me if I confine my letter to what is necessary. In the first place, Mrs. Blackburn spoke of forwarding me some boots. If you can do so I should be very much obliged, for those I have completely worn out. In the second place, principally owing to my boots being worn through, my socks are likewise beyond repair.....Can you send me a razor? I shall have to shave myself here I think, and it would, of course, be a saving of expense in the long run. Any kind of razor would do for me; I have shaved with a dissecting scalpel before now. I would solve the difficulty by not shaving at all, if it were possible for me to grow a beard: but repeated experiment has convinced me that the only result of such action is to make me look like an escaped convict...I am not at present capable if writing; but it would be an absolute mercy to have any books. At present there is nothing to keep my mind from dwelling on itself. I may say I shall want even a Shakespeare for the Dublin article, since I believe they have not one here. I could easily find distraction for my mind there. And with regard to my illness there is nothing to be alarmed about. It is severer and more obstinate than I had hoped would be the case; but it is a mere matter of holding on. And in that kind of passive endurance I am well practiced. I daresay this week will see the end of it......I think I shall like this place when I begin again to like anything. The want of books is the principal drawback so far as I see at present. Let me say that I keep on my legs and force myself to go out as much as possible.... Please accept my warmest thanks for all your kindness and trouble on my behalf. I know this is a very perfunctory-looking letter, but until the first sharp struggle is over, it is difficult for me to write in any other way. Once again however, there is no cause at all for uneasiness on that account.[1]

Elizabeth Blackburn, mentioned by Thompson at the head of his letter, worked frequently for both Wilfrid and Alice Meynell as a proof reader, regularly becoming their chief collaborator on many of their journals. Thompson would call her, Madam, earned so he always maintained for her tendency to manage his affairs. While occasionally irritated by her interference, he tolerated it on account of her genuine affection for him. He always respected her often outspoken and critical views while agreeing to differ. Her son, Vernon[2], a noted music critic and author of books on Bayreuth and Felix Mendelssohn, was also a prominent journalist in Catholic circles, having been the Rome editor of *The Tablet* and Music Critic for *The Pall Mall Gazette*.

Settling into a daily routine that involved the discipline of regular writing, most of his completed contributions at this time were review essays based on recently published books. He also submitted an article on Macbeth to *The Dublin Review*. Soon, after his arrival, he would assemble one his greatest creations, *Ode to the Setting Sun*. It was while standing alongside a life-size crucifix in a field owned by the Priory, just as the sun went down over Kithurst Hill, that he began to feel, *"soul, sky, and music blend together"*. Under the shadow of the crucifix he began his Ode and within a few days a fair copy was made and sent off to London. It was perhaps the first sign of his poetic maturity:

> Alpha and Omega, sadness and mirth,
> The springing music, and its wasting breath-
> The fairest things in life are Death and Birth,
> And of these two the fairer thing is Death.
> Mystical twins of Time inseparable,
> The younger hath the holier array,
> And hath the awfuller sway:
> It is the falling star that trails the light,
> It is the breaking wave that hath the might,
> The passing shower that rainbows maniple.
> Is it not so, O thou down-stricken Day,
> That draw'st thy splendours round thee in thy fall?

The Meynell family, busy as they always were, most notably with the construction of their new house, were astounded with what they received, taking time out in July to visit the poet at his Sussex base. The work was duly published in the September edition of *Merry England*. A delighted Meynell now sought further recognition for his protégé, sending examples of his poetry to, among others, Tennyson and Browning. Tennyson responded somewhat cautiously through his son, but Browning, a long-standing friend of the Meynell family replied most warmly, his letter subsequently being published in the January 1890 edition of *Merry England* as an example of the older poet's generosity toward an unknown writer:

> I hardly know how to apologize to you, or to explain to myself how there has occurred such a delay in doing what I had an impulse to do as soon as I read the very interesting papers written by Francis Thompson and so kindly brought under my notice by yourself. Both the verse and the prose are indeed remarkable.....Pray assure him, if he cares to know it, that I shall have a confident expectation of his success if he will but extricate himself-as by a strenuous effort he may-from all that must now embarrass him terribly...

A further reaction came from a rather unexpected quarter, the poet's uncle, Edward Healy Thompson:

> I have followed Francis's literary course with much interest, and I have read the Ode more than once, and on perusal have found it more intelligible-for I confess that some passages were beyond my comprehension, but probably from not understanding the allusions. He has great command of diction, and no doubt the composition is overloaded with imagery, but then how gorgeous was the subject. There are lines that live in one's memory and have a wonderful music of their own.[3]

While often deeply depressed amid the relative isolation of Storrington, Thompson took to joining the village children in their walks throughout the locality. One child, Daisy Stanford, named like her sisters, Rose, Lily and Violet after flowers, became a favourite of the poet. He would often join her in picking the wild raspberries that grew on Kithurst Hill, as well as all around the foot of Jacob's Ladder. She had no idea that she would become the stimulus for one of his finest poems, *Daisy*. While the work represents a total contrast to his *Ode To The Setting Sun*, the two together, one complex, the other more simplistic in outlook, show him, now free of the influence of drugs, continuing to develop in artistic terms:

Where the thistle lifts a purple crown
    Six foot out of the turf,
And the harebell shakes on the windy hill-
    O the breath of the distant surf!-

The hills look over on the South,
    And southward dreams the sea;
And, with the sea-breeze hand in hand,
    Came innocence and she.

Where 'mid the gorse the raspberry
    Red for the gatherer springs,
Two children did we stray and talk
    Wise, idle, childish things.

She listened with big-lipped surprise,
    Breast-deep 'mid flower and spine:
Her skin was like a grape, whose veins
    Run snow instead of wine.

She knew not those sweet words she spake,
Nor knew her own sweet way;
But there's never a bird, so sweet a song
Thronged in whose throat that day!

Oh, there were flowers in Storrington
On the turf and on the spray;
But the sweetest flower on Sussex hills
Was the Daisy-flower that day!

Her beauty smoothed earth's furrowed face!
She gave me tokens three:-
A look, a word of her winsome mouth,
And a wild raspberry.

A berry red, a guileless look,
A still word,-strings of sand!
And yet they made my wild, wild heart
Fly down to her little hand.

For, standing artless as the air,
And candid as the skies,
She took the berries with her hand,
And the love with her sweet eyes.

The fairest things have fleetest end:
Their scent survives their close,
But the rose's scent is bitterness
To him that loved the rose!

She looked a little wistfully,
Then went her sunshine way:-
The sea's eye had a mist on it,
And the leaves fell from the day.

She went her unremembering way,
She went and left in me
The pang of all the partings gone,
And partings yet to be.

She left me marvelling why my soul
Was sad that she was glad;
At all the sadness in the sweet,
The sweetness in the sad.

Still, still I seemed to see her, still
Look up with soft replies,
And take the berries with her hand,
And the love with her lovely eyes.

Nothing begins, and nothing ends,
That is not paid with moan;
For we are born in other's pain,
And perish in our own.

Bishop Vaughan, who had known Thompson when a pupil at Ushaw, after meeting him in later years at the Meynell family home, had suggested that he write something for *The Dublin Review*, which the priest owned, but did not edit. The result was an extended essay, some ten thousand words long, on the work of the Romantic poet, Percy Bysshe Shelley. Spending the long Autumn months totally preoccupied with the project, Thompson submitted the completed work to Wilfrid Meynell who thought it splendid. Most surprisingly, the editor of *The Dublin Review* rejected the work. In a letter to his old friend Canon Carroll, a somewhat irate Thompson gave vent to his frustrations:

> The article on Shelley which you asked about I finished at last, with quite agonising pain and elaboration. It might have been written in tears and is proportionately dear to me. I fear, however, that it will not be accepted, or accepted only with such modifications as will go to my heart. It has not been inserted in the current issue of the Dublin-a fact which looks ominous. First, you see, I prefaced it by a fiery attack on Catholic Philistinism, driven home with all the rhetoric I could muster. That is pretty sure to be a stumbling-block. I consulted Mr Meynell as to its suppression, but he said "Leave it in." Secondly, it is written at an almost incessant level of poetic prose, and seethes with imagery like my poetry itself. Now the sober, ponderous, ecclesiastical Dublin confronted with poetic prose must be considerably scared. The editor cannot make up his mind whether it is heavenly rhetoric or infernal nonsense.[4]

Discovered among Thompson's papers following his death, the essay was subsequently published by Wilfrid Ward, the then editor of *The Dublin Review* in the July issue of 1908. Such was its impact, that for the first time in its long and illustrious history the magazine went into a second edition. The literary critic of *The Observer* lauded it as, *"a memorable masterpiece of English prose"*. Later published as a separate booklet by Burns and Oates, together with an introduction by the Right Honourable George Wyndham, it has subsequently been reprinted on numerous occasions. Indeed, there are countless learned critics who view it as his greatest work, many considering it far superior to any of his poetry.

In *The Sere of the Leaf*, a poem also written at Storrington, Thompson is again struggling to make his poetry a substitute for reality amid the innumerable tensions overwhelming him while still in remission. The work, with its many Celtic influences, began its life following the first of many meetings with the Irish poet, Katharine Tynan, over the years a regular visitor to the Meynell household. Her pleasing demeanour greatly impressed Thompson, as did her poetry. For her part, she delighted in Thompson's conversation, the two spending many hours together deep in religious and philosophical debate. In later years, becoming one of Thompson's greatest enthusiasts, she did much to bring his poetry to a wider audience, courtesy of her reviews published in the *Irish Independent*.

Having completed his essay on *Shelley*, and feeling better in himself, both mentally and physically, throughout December 1889, Thompson began work on early sketches for *The Hound of Heaven*. It was duly completed three months later. Individual elements had flitted in and out of his subconscious for almost a year. However, it was not until he made the huge leap to the concept of God as a relentlessly pursuing cosmic hound that everything then quickly fell into place. While over the years, many have been quick to point out that much of the imagery and thought can be traced to numerous external influences, the central unifying element is purely and simply Francis Thompson himself.

By now, Thompson had become more and more frustrated with the loneliness and isolation of Storrington and sought a return to London. With Wilfrid Meynell still constantly subsidising his living costs, the poet became determined to repay his debts by participating in the Meynell's many journalistic enterprises. As always, Meynell was hugely wary of Thompson's possible return to live in the capital with all its many temptations. Thompson himself was particularly bullish: *"Nor need you fear the opium. I have learned the advantage of being without it for mental exercise; and (still more important) I have learned to bear my fits of depression without it. Personally, I no longer fear it!"*[5]

Rooms were found for him at No 25 Third Avenue, Queen's Park, Kilburn. There he would work on *The Hound of Heaven* as well as going on to compile a short story, *Finis Coronat Opus*. Working closely in tandem with Alice Meynell, the pair soon became highly proficient at producing whatever magazine copy was required by deadline day. While in the last twelve months, Thompson had produced only half dozen articles and five published poems, very soon he would complete some thirty poems, review at least sixteen volumes of verse, more than a dozen other book reviews and produce a twenty five thousand word study of the work of St John Baptist de La Salle, that would occupy the entire April 1891 edition of *Merry England.*

Twice Meynell prevailed upon Thompson to provide some obituary verse. The first occasion was the death, in August, 1890, of Cardinal Newman. Initially hesitant, within the space of a few hours, however, he had compiled three stanzas that appeared in *The Register* of 16th August. The second occasion, following the death of Cardinal Manning in January, 1892, saw him produce the highly impressive, *To The Dead Cardinal of Westminster*, published in the February edition of *Merry England*. Not everything enjoyed success, *A Threnody of Birth*, together with an article entitled *Modern Men: The Devil*, earned the displeasure of the distinguished editor of *The Observer*, William Ernest Henley.

Perhaps the outstanding work of this period remains *Sister Songs*. When visiting Palace Court, daughter Monica Meynell had entered the room just as the two men were talking of Daisy Stanford, the original inspiration of his Storrington poem. Meynell inquired of Thompson if Daisy was taller than Monica: *"Mr Thompson has a friend called Daisy and he has written some beautiful poetry to her, which I wish had been written for you, my dear!"*[6] That casual remark seems to have lit a spark in the poet's imagination, who, in a delightful gesture, eventually placed his completed manuscript of *Sister Songs* on the Meynell's mantlepiece, to be discovered just as the family exchanged their gifts at Christmas, 1891.

As the family rejoiced in their new home, Palace Court, here again filled to the rafters with books, the Clan Meynell were *"at home"* every Sunday evening. Open house was kept for anyone interested in poetry and literature, but also for the leading artists and other *"interesting people"* of the day. There were regular poetry readings, music recitals and constant literary talk. As always Thompson was included, though his comings and goings were always unexpected, for he never seemed to have any semblance of time. Everyone overlooked his untied bootlaces, the oversized collar, the overcoat worn forgetfully throughout dinner, or the smoke billowing forth from a smouldering pipe in his pocket.

Sadly, it was not too long after Thompson's return to London that a crisis occurred. Entering their library late one evening, Wilfrid and Alice found Thompson lying on the floor amid a highly disturbing opium stupor. Despite his excuses, the couple, worried about their children's reaction, told the poet in no uncertain terms that his visits to their house should cease immediately. A distraught Thompson then went back to spending his nights as a penniless vagrant on the benches along the Embankment. Eventually located by Meynell, the solution agreed after discussions with the poet, was another period of isolation far away from London. His new home would soon be a remote Franciscan Monastery at Pantasaph in North Wales.

Thus, in late December, 1891, a day or two after his thirty second birthday, Thompson was sent-off to the mother house of the English Province of the Capuchin Friars Minor, their brown habits girded with the white chord of Saint Francis and known as "the bearded counsellors of God." The date was decided by H.A. Hinkson, the husband of Katharine Tynan, who offered to accompany Francis as far as Chester. Clad as usual in his brown ulster and bowler hat, his few possessions crammed into a small carpet bag, Thompson and Hinkson spent the journey talking cricket. The arrival in the carriage of Irish navvies, one with a badly cut hand, allowed Thompson to recall his medical training as he expertly cleaned and bandaged the wound. A Friar from the monastery was waiting to accompany him on the final part of the journey from Chester.

Three miles from Holywell in Flintshire, and more a district than a village, Pantasaph is named after a hollow or "pant" at the base of a hill and the local saint whose holy well further down the valley is commemorated by Great Britain's second smallest city, St Asaph. The highly impressive Gothic buildings of the monastery, dating from 1852, lie at the end of a long tree-lined lane. Staying first at Bishop's House and then in a cottage behind the monastery, Thompson's final residence there was Creccas Cottage with its magnificent views of Mount Snowdon. Removed once again from the temptation of opium for a period of almost five years, although little did he realise it, this was to be his last real surge of creative writing.

Originally part of the estate of Lady Fielding whose husband, Lord Fielding, later became the Earl of Denbigh, at that time Protestants with high church leanings, they proposed to build a church on their property. Soon after the laying of the foundation stone in August, 1849, however, the couple became Catholics, strongly desiring their church be devoted to Catholic worship. Shortly after it was completed, the couple presented it to the Capuchins as their first English foundation. Upon their arrival on 25 October, 1852, the little community was housed in the rectory, which later became the guest house. There they continued to live until 1865 when the present monastery was formally opened. The following year Pantasaph was made the Capuchin Novitiate for Great Britain.

Thompson's first few days, amid appallingly bad weather, were spent indoors. Having already experienced the withdrawal symptoms from his addiction, early in January he was able to report to Meynell, *"C'en est fait, as regards the opium."* Staying first in the guest house, Bishop's House, there he was made most welcome by the large family of its proprietor, Michael Brien. These included five girls and a teenage son. The youngest of the Brien offspring was eight year Agnes, while the oldest was Margaret Ann, a twenty four year old softly spoken girl whose health was not always robust. Thompson was immediately attracted to her and writes about her in his very first epistle from his Welsh hideaway:

> Now you'll think that I am in a state of light-hearted exhilarence, which is very improper in me, considering all I have to repent of. Therefore I beg to assure you that I'm suffering like old Nick. But when one is in this condition, one must laugh out or weep out.....therefore I'll grin through the very biggest horse-collar I can find. Don't think though that I repent having come here: if I were in London I would simply take a header into the Thames-only it's such a damnably dirty place for a poet to drown in. But I am in a most unconventional state at present; ready to go smash all conventions like a bull in a china shop....I have half a mind, by way of final outrage to make love to what I think the loveliest girl I have ever seen. But I have still some convention about me in a tattered condition.....[7]

While there, falling increasingly in love with nature, on more than one occasion it is known that he would often spend all night out of doors. A favourite trip for Thompson would be a walk through the extensive woods surrounding the monastery and taking in a visit to the nearby town of Holywell, home to St Winefride's Well. This venerable Christian shrine is the only one in Britain with a record of pilgrimage that stretches back 1,000 years. The spring that feeds the well is said to have burst miraculously from the spot where St Winefride, in defence of her chastity, was slain by Caradoc, son of an Amorican prince in about the year 634. Pilgrims still flock to what has become known as the Lourdes of Wales, particularly on the nearest Sunday to June 22, St Winefride's Day. Above the Well remains a chapel built by the munificence of Lady Margaret, the mother of King Henry VII.

Such walks were invariably taken in the company of Father Anselm, a twenty eight year old philosophy teacher and editor of the Order's official Magazine, *Franciscan Annals*. Labelled by Thompson as a "friend, philosopher and guide," this very personification of Franciscan simplicity later became Archbishop Kenealy of Simla. Anselm, fully aware of Thompson's long record of drug abuse had been assigned to keep an eye on him. They soon talked long and enthusiastically about philosophical and religious matters, Anselm amazed at both the range and breadth of his new companion's knowledge. Many of their conversations were first channelled by Anselm into the pages of his magazine before, in 1931, recalling the poet more fully in the Franciscan periodical, *Carmina*. Two years later, he expanded his reminiscences for *The Capuchin Annual*:

> He was not much of a man to look at. Slightly under middle height, his face was redeemed from the commonplace by a fine and spacious forehead, a splendid pair of large grey eyes that seemed always changing into light blue, a small but definitely combative nose and the orator's mouth of no particular symmetry. About his whole appearance there was a suggestion of physical frailness, yet withal of nervous energy and grace from his delicate features to the tips of his artistic fingers.
>
> He was gentle of manner and during all the years I knew him I never once heard a harsh word fall from his lips. Though unimpressive in figure he was a wonder when he opened his mouth to talk. His language was virile and flowing. He would, indeed, to his intimated friends, both speak and write at times with a phraseological pomp that was hardly justified by the subject.
>
> His career was a lament of unpunctualities. He thought and read and wrote at night when he should have been asleep. He slept far into the day when he should have been up and doing.[8]

The poet had a similar effect on the Honourable Everard Feilding, who with a friend, having called on the poet at Pantasaph at five one evening found him still asleep in bed. He called back an hour later, again without success. Leaving a note inviting Thompson to breakfast at 9.30 a.m., the following morning, the meeting duly took place as Fielding later related:

> Instead of parables in polysyllables and a riot of imagery, we found simplicity and modesty and a manner which would have been commonplace if it had not been so sincere. But the charm and interest of his talk grew with the night, and it was already dawn when we escorted him back across the snow to his untimely meal. He told us, I remember, of his poetic development, and of how, until recently, he had fancied that the end of poetry was reached in the striking together of ingenious images, an art in which, he somewhat naively confessed, he know himself to excel; but that now he knew it should reach further, and he hoped for an improvement in his future work.[9]

Soon after his arrival, as Thompson knelt at the Christmas crib in the Pantasaph chapel, he began the creation of one of his most delightful works, *Little Jesus*. It moved from an initial draft of some eighteen lines being further expanded to fifty. Struck by the simplicity of Franciscan life, the poem appears driven by the all-pervading atmosphere of the monastery, rather than just the crib. Completed by the end of March, as was a companion piece, the sonnet, *Desiderium Indesideratum*, Thompson seems to have cast them aside at the time. Little else followed for a few months save for *Any Saint*. Thompson himself was more than preoccupied with the attractions of Maggie Brien.

A slim, lively young woman with large appealing eyes and deep brown hair, her many duties included helping her mother around the house and also looking after their guests. While a mutual shyness undoubtedly slowed the courtship initially, over the coming months the relationship developed and deepened. Throughout the next two years, as Thompson embarked on his first mature love affair, his artistic creativity began to take a huge leap forward. From this period comes the powerful, *An Anthem of Earth*, while, *A Narrow Vessel*, fully records the affair, as does the even more explicit but unpublished verses he called, *La Marguerite*, a title he later deleted in favour of *Wild-Flower*.

However, Maggie's coquettish and light-hearted behaviour often annoyed the more serious-minded Thompson. The affair seems to have lasted, on and off, until well into 1895. By the middle of 1894, the Briens had given up running Bishop's House and moved to nearby Creccas Cottage. This was situated just over the hill behind the monastery. In October of that year, Thompson, having quarrelled with his new landlady, went to live on his own at nearby Ivy Cottage. However, by the July of the following year, he had again moved in with the Brien family, but now at Creccas Cottage. Despite its cramped conditions, he occupied a combined bedroom and sitting room on the first floor.

By the time Thompson eventually left Pantasaph to return to London in 1896, despite living together in the same house, the couple's relationship had long since cooled. Never marrying, Maggie herself lived out her life in Pantasaph. Having returned from church on the morning of Sunday, October 7th, 1907, just three weeks before Thompson's death, she died suddenly of a heart attack. She was buried in an unmarked grave in the monastery's churchyard. A long time afterwards her family discovered a faded and yellowing photograph of the poet tucked behind another picture in her room. Even as late as 1964, Maggie's sister, Agnes, still spoke most warmly of their special relationship.

In the interim, Thompson had received news from Wilfrid Meynell regarding the publication of a volume of his poetry, simply entitled *Poems*. First appearing in November, 1893, this almost square book of eighty one pages carried a frontispiece by Laurence Housman, visualizing part of *The Hound of Heaven*. By skilful use of the Browning letter, while emphasising Thompson's somewhat Bohemian background, Meynell had very astutely attracted much pre-publication publicity. Of all the many volumes of poetry published throughout the 1890s, none aroused attention such as this. It went through three editions in its first three months, earning enormous sums in royalties. A new poet had duly arrived!

From the intellectual ferment fostered by his friendship with Father Anselm and the other monks, together with his total abstinence from drugs, Thompson felt a fresh urge to compose. The most immediate results were *Any Saint, Assumpta Maria* and *From the Night of Forebeing*. This new creative period would last until the turn of the new century. Becoming increasingly dissatisfied with his earlier work, Thompson, with Father Anselm's help, now sought to add a far greater degree of philosophical depth to his often unrelenting use of language. Such a dramatic change in outlook undoubtedly coincided with the advent of his friendship with the poet, Coventry Patmore.

The son of a journalist, Coventry Kersey Dighton Patmore was born at Woodford in Essex in 1823. He had little formal education apart from a few months at the Collège de France in 1839. Six years later, with his father on the run from his creditors, Patmore was left very much to his own devices. A period of journalism followed before, thanks to the patronage of Lord Houghton, he was nominated for a position in the Printed Books Department of the British Museum. He would work there for nineteen years. In the meantime, it was down to his continued friendship with Alfred Lord Tennyson, particularly between 1846 and 1862, that saw him find his own distinctive poetic voice.

Thanks to his epic of married love, *The Angel in the House*, by the middle of the nineteenth century, Coventry Patmore had become one of the best known poets in England. Having taken up the form of the irregular ode, soon, however, his poetry explored mystical philosophy, rather obscure theology and much metrical experimentation. Alice Meynell particularly came to adore him, as did Edmund Gosse. To her, his poetry was "the greatest thing in the world, the most harrowing and the sweetest. I can hardly realise that he who has written it and who is greater than his words is celestially kind to me and calls me a friend." If it was good enough for Alice, it was good enough for Thompson.

Thompson's own acquaintance with Patmore's work had begun while he was at Storrington in 1889. Though his initial response was somewhat lukewarm, twelve months later, thanks to Alice, he was prepared to accept Patmore as, "the great Catholic poet whom it has been the desire of my life to see." It was not, however, until Patmore's review of *Poems* in 1894, that Thompson accepted the older poet as a guide and mentor. A few months later, Meynell sent him Patmore's second collection of essays for review together with a copy of his book, *Religio Poetae*. While completing his article, Thompson began a correspondence with his fellow poet, setting in train a whole series of meetings.

Patmore, who as a member of the Third Order of St Francis, visited Pantasaph during October, 1894. It was that visit that set the seal on the pair's relationship both personal and poetic. Amid unrelenting intellectual debates, the two found much to discuss, and having spent two years in somewhat splendid isolation, Thompson found his visitor hugely stimulating company. Expressing a special sympathy for Thompson's drug problems, having once defended Coleridge's use of laudanum, Patmore revealed that he himself had even experimented with hashish. From that day, they began a regular correspondence that lasted until Patmore's sudden death in 1896. For the rest of his life, Thompson would revere Coventry Patmore as, *"the greatest genius of the century"*.

During these two years, from 1894 until 1896, Thompson created more than a dozen poems, all of which bear the distinctive stamp of Patmore's influence. Such as *Orient Ode*, *From the Night of Forebeing* and *The Dread of Height*, all have typical fingerprints, while *The Mistress of Vision*, perhaps remains the most Patmorean of all. For many, however, only once during Thompson's Pantasaph days did the poet write with the full impact of his old power and that was in *An Anthem of Earth*. Here, amid his attempt to depict the intellectual and emotional progress of Man from birth until death, most critics trace not the influences of Coventry Patmore, but that of William Shakespeare.

To be able to capitalise on the success of the earlier volume of Thompson's *Poems*, late in 1894, Meynell urged the publication of *Sister Songs*, which Thompson, after some initial hesitation, eventually agreed to. Thus, in December, 1894, he returned to London to prepare the manuscript, *Sister Songs* eventually being published in June, 1895. Surprisingly, sales were disappointing, with under six hundred copies sold in the first six months. Thompson's initial reaction had perhaps been the right one. However, despite the early reaction, his publishers were keen to publish yet another collection of his work. Back at Pantasaph, Thompson was hard at work fashioning his *New Poems*.

Writing to Alice Meynell in June, 1896, somewhat exhausted as he neared completion of the project, the poet gave vent to the great strain he was under:

> The whole book I look back to as a bad dream, so unexampled in my previous experience was the labour I bestowed on it. Indeed, during the last six months, over and above the rewriting of the poems which were ready to hand, I must have written about thirty new poems, long and short: for there were not above twenty or so when I began the book. I hardly wrote more than thirty in the whole five years preceding my first book, so that it was an unprecedented strain for me.[10]

Much of the content of this collection was in fact drawn from works already written, eight of which had appeared in *Merry England*, the magazine itself finally closing later that year. The numerous reworked drafts show Thompson aiming more at both economy and clarity, putting both perhaps above poetic sensibility. By far the most important section was *Sight and Insight*, five existing poems, together with seven new works created during the months of preparation. Two others, *Carmen Genesis* and *Ad Castitatem*, perhaps rather unwisely, were added by Meynell in his role of General Editor. By April, having finally completed his work on *New Poems*, without warning, Thompson was the recipient of further dramatic news.

Having had only occasional dealings with his estranged father, while at Pantasaph, on 8th April, 1896, Thompson received the sad message that Dr Charles Thompson lay close to death from congestion of the lungs. He was aged 72. Having caught a cold on Good Friday, his condition worsened over Easter, until pneumonia took hold. Borrowing money at the monastery, Thompson hastily brought a return ticket to Manchester and then made his way to Ashton-under-Lyne. Tragically, if not untypically, he had arrived too late, his father having died the previous night. Refused accommodation at the family home in Stamford Street by his step mother, thanks to the kindness of friends, Thompson resided at St Peter's Rectory in nearby Stalybridge.

Though making little contact with his family, Thompson stayed on to attend his father's funeral on the 13th April. A day later he stopped-off to see his sister, Mary, for the very last time, at her convent in nearby Manchester. She later wrote to Wilfrid Meynell telling him that Thompson, "could see his old friends were unable to shake off their former notions of him and believe him changed." Almost seventy years later, when contacted by the author, John Walsh, the poet's much younger half-brother, Norbert Thompson, born in 1891, stated that he had been warned by his mother to avoid any rudeness to their visitor[11]. Despite barely speaking to one another, each gazing at the other in open curiosity, Norbert never ever forgot the blotched and sallow skin of Francis Thompson's sad and mournful face. The memory stayed with him for the rest of his life.

Inserted in the prayer book Thompson retained for the rest of his life, a mortuary card was later found. It read - Offer your charity and pray for the soul of Charles Thompson, M.R.C.S., L.S.A., who departed this life, April 9th 1896, aged 72, fortified by the rites of Holy Church - The silent and wise man shall be honoured. Amid all the poet's gloom however, that very same month, *The Edinburgh Review* had published an article describing him as an already great poet who could become even greater. Such praise helped lift his spirits as he returned to work on the completion of his *New Poems*.

Chapter 4

THE HOUND OF HEAVEN

I fled Him, down the nights and down the days;
I fled Him down the arches of the years;
I fled Him, down the labyrinthine ways
Of my own mind; and in the mist of tears
I hid from Him, and under running laughter.
Up vistaed hopes I sped;
And shot, precipitated
Adown Titanic glooms of chasmed fears,
From those strong Feet that followed, followed after.
But with unhurrying chase,
And unperturbéd pace,
Deliberate speed, majestic instancy,
They beat – and a Voice beat
More instant than the Feet –
"All things betray thee, who betrayest Me."

I pleaded, outlaw-wise,
By many a hearted casement, curtained red,
Trellised with intertwining charities;
(For, though I knew His love Who followéd
Yet was I sore adread
Lest, having Him, I must have naught beside)
But, if one little casement parted wide,
The gust of His approach would clash it to.
Fear wist not to evade, as Love wist to pursue.
Across the margent of the world I fled,
And troubled the gold gateways of the stars,
Fretted to dulcet jars

And silvern clatter the pale ports o' the moon,
I said to dawn: Be sudden-to eve: Be soon;
With thy young skiey blossoms heap me over
From this tremendous Lover!
Float thy vague veil about me, lest He see!
I tempted all His servitors, but to find
My own betrayal in their constancy,
In faith to Him their fickleness to me,
Their traitorous trueness, and their loyal deceit.
To all swift things for swiftness did I sue;
Clung to the whistling mane of every wind.
But whether they swept, smoothly fleet,
The long savannahs of the blue;
Or whether, Thunder-driven,
They clanged his chariot 'thwart a heaven,
Plashy with flying lightnings round the spurn o' their feet:-
Fear wist not to evade as Love wist to pursue.
Still with unhurrying chase,
And unperturbèd pace,
Deliberate speed, majestic instancy.
Came on the following Feet,
And a voice above their beat–
"Naught shelters thee, who wilt not shelter Me."

I sought no more that, after which I strayed,
In face of man or maid;
But still within the little childrens' eyes
Seems something, something that replies;
They at least are for me, surely forme!
I turned me to them very wistfully;
But just as their young eyes grew sudden fair
With dawning answers there,
Their angel plucked them from me by the hair.
"Come then, ye other children, Nature's – share
With me" (said I) "your delicate fellowship;
Let me greet you lip to lip,
Let me twine with you caresses,
Wantoning
With our Lady-Mother's vagrant tresses,
Banqueting
With her in her wind-walled palace,
Underneath her azured dais,
Quaffing, as your taintless way is,
From a chalice

Members of the Meynell family at Palace Court.
From left to right: Madeline, Everard, Viola, Alice, Wilfrid, Olivia and Francis.

Alice Meynell

47 Palace Court, Bayswater

Storrington Priory

Creccas Cottage at Pantasaph

Maggie and Agnes Brien

Coventry Patmore

Katie King

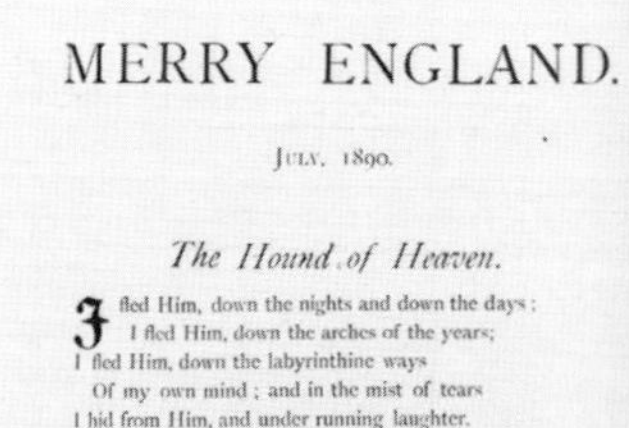

MERRY ENGLAND.

JULY, 1890.

The Hound of Heaven.

I fled Him, down the nights and down the days;
I fled Him, down the arches of the years;
I fled Him, down the labyrinthine ways
Of my own mind; and in the mist of tears
I hid from Him, and under running laughter.
Up vistaed hopes I sped;
And shot, precipitated
Adown Titanic glooms of chasmed fears,
From those strong Feet that followed, followed after.
But with unhurrying chase,
And unperturbèd pace,
Deliberate speed, majestic instancy,
They beat—and a Voice beat
More instant than the Feet—
"All things betray thee, who betrayest Me."

I pleaded, outlaw-wise,
By many a hearted casement, curtained red,
Trellised with intertwining charities;
(For, though I knew His love Who followèd
Yet was I sore adread
Lest, having Him, I must have naught beside)

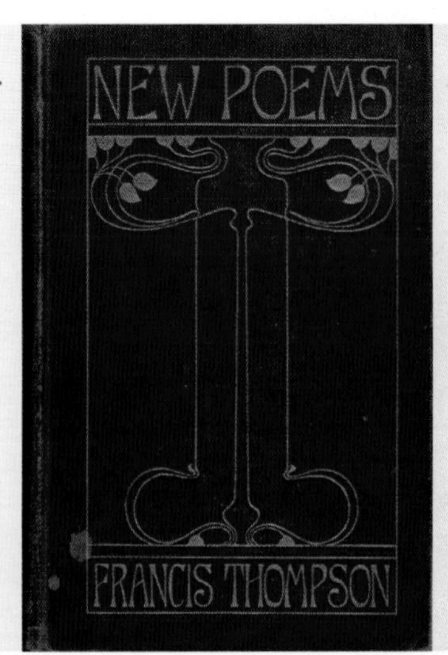

POEMS
BY FRANCIS
THOMPSON

LONDON AND NEW YORK
JOHN LANE, THE BODLEY HEAD

First publication of The Hound of Heaven in Merry England. Covers of published poetry.

E.V. Lucas

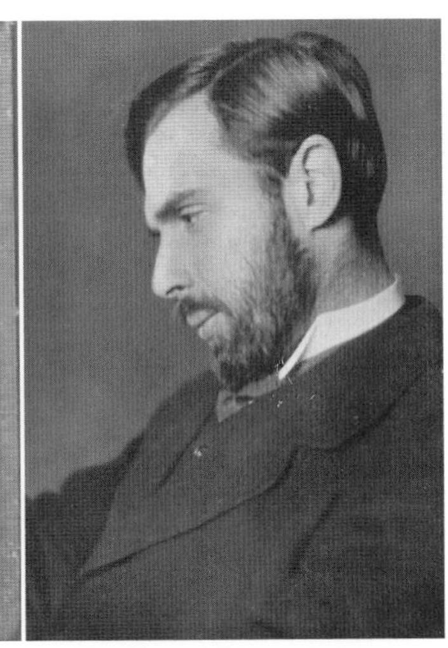

Everard Meynell

Maurice Jacobson

Fartein Valen

Sir William Harris

Howard Blake

The Hound of Heaven

For Tenor Solo, S.A.T.B. and Orchestra

Words by

FRANCIS THOMPSON

Set to Music by

MAURICE JACOBSON

CURWEN EDITION 3735

Vocal Score 8/6

LONDON : J. CURWEN & SONS LTD., 24 BERNERS STREET, W.1
NEW YORK : G. SCHIRMER INC., SOLE AGENTS FOR U.S.A.

Made in England

Ronald Corp

Sketch by Everard Meynell, 1907

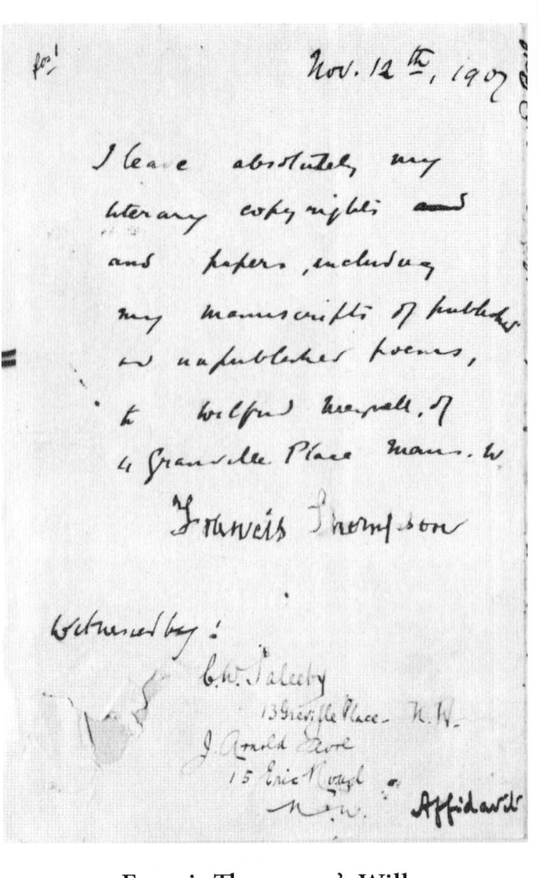

Nov. 12th, 1907

I leave absolutely my literary copyrights and and papers, including my manuscripts of published or unpublished poems, to Wilfrid Meynell, of 4 Granville Place Mans. W.

Francis Thompson

Witnessed by:
C.W. Saleeby
13 Greville Place N.W.
J. Arnold [illegible]
15 Eric Road
N.W.

Affidavit

Francis Thompson's Will

to the memory of
FRANCIS THOMPSON, POET
1859–1907
STUDENT OF OWENS COLLEGE
1877–1884
Whatso looks lovelily
Is but the rainbow on life's weeping rain.
Why have we longings of immortal pain,
And all we long for mortal? Woe is me,
And all our chants but chaplet some decay,
As mine this vanishing—nay vanished day.

Memorial Plaque, Manchester, carved by Eric Gill

Kensal Green Cemetery

Memorial Plaque, Harris Museum, Preston

Lucent-weeping out of the dayspring."
So it was done:
I in their delicate fellowship was one-
Drew the bolt of Nature's secrecies.
I knew all the swift importings
On the wilful face of skies;
I knew how the clouds arise
Spumèd of the wild sea-snortings;
All that's born or dies
Rose and drooped with–made them shapers
Of mine own moods, or wailful or divine-
With them joyed and was bereaven.
I was heavy with the even,
When she lit her glimmering tapers
Round the day's dead sanctities.
I laughed in the morning's eyes.
I triumphed and I saddened with all weather,
Heaven and I wept together,
And its sweet tears were salt with mortal mine;
Against the red throb of its sunset-heart
I laid my own to beat,
And sharecommingling heat;
But not by that, by that, was eased my human smart.
In vain my tears were wet on Heaven's grey cheek.
For ah! we know not what each other says,
These things and I; in sound I speak–
Their sound is but their stir, they speak by silences.
Nature, poor stepdame, cannot slake my drouth;
Let her, if she would owe me,
Drop yon blue bosom-veil of sky, and show me
The breasts o' her tenderness:
Never did any milk of hers once bless
My thirsting mouth.
Nigh and nigh draws the chase,
With unperturbèd pace,
Deliberate speed, majestic instancy:
And past those noisèd Feet
A Voice comes yet more fleet–
"Lo! naught contents thee, who content'st not Me."

Naked I wait Thy love's uplifted stroke!
My harness piece by piece Thou hast hewn from me,
And smitten me to my knee;
I am defenceless utterly.

I slept, methinks, and woke,
And, slowly gazing, find me stripped in sleep.
In the rash lustihead of my young powers,
I shook the pillaring hours
And pulled my life upon me; grimed with smears,
I stand amid the dust o' the mounded years–
My mangled youth lies dead beneath the heap.
My days have crackled and gone up in smoke,
Have puffed and burst as sun-starts on a stream.
Yea, faileth now even dream
The dreamer, and the lute the lutanist;
Even the linked fantasies, in whose blossomly twist
I swung the earth a trinket at my wrist,
Are yielding; what availed they ever? I grazed
Too closely Thy blue window as I gazed,
Jutted a careless elbow through clear Heaven
And gashed me with the splinters-see I bleed.
Ah! is Thy love indeed
A weed, albeit an amaranthine weed,
Suffering no flowers except its own to mount?
Ah! must–
Designer infinite!–
Ah! must Thou char the wood ere Thou canst limn with it?
My freshness spent its wavering shower i' the dust;
And now my heart is as a broken fount,
Wherein tear-drippings stagnate, spilt down ever
From the dank thoughts that shiver
Upon the sighful branches of my mind.
Such is; what is to be?
The pulp so bitter, how shall taste the rind?
I dimly guess what Time in mists confounds;
Yet ever and anon a trumpet sounds
From the hid battlements of Eternity,
Those shaken mists a space unsettle, then
Round the half-glimpséd turrets slowly wash again;
But not ere him who summoneth
I first have seen, enwound
With glooming robes purpureal, cypress-crowned;
His name I know, and what his trumpet saith.
Whether man's heart or life it be which yields
Thee harvest, must Thy harvest fields
Be dunged with rotten death?
Now of that long pursuit
Comes on at hand the bruit;

That Voice is round me like a bursting sea:
"And is thy earth so marred,
Shattered in shard on shard?
Lo, all things fly thee, for thou fliest Me!
"Strange, piteous, futile thing!
Wherefore should any set thee love apart?
Seeing none but I makes much of naught" (He said).
"And human love needs human meriting:
How hast thou merited–
Of all man's clotted clay the dingiest clot?
Alack, thou knowest not
How little worthy of any love thou art!
Whom wilt thou find to love ignoble thee.
Save Me, save only Me?
All which I took from thee I did but take,
Not for thy harms,
But just that thou might'st seek it in My arms.
All which thy child's mistake
Fancies as lost, I have stored for thee at home:
Rise, clasp My hand, and come."

Halts by me that footfall:
Is my gloom, after all,
Shade of His hand, outstretched caressingly?
"Ah, fondest, blindest, weakest,
I am He Whom thou seekest!
Thou dravest love from thee, who dravest Me."[1]

In June 1890, subscribers to Wilfrid Meynell's still rather niche English Catholic magazine, *Merry England*, found themselves looking at this new, somewhat strange, and even disturbing poem, by a then little-known English poet, Francis Thompson. Having overcome an almost Shakespearian catalogue of tragic circumstances in his life, he was then tucked away in a Sussex monastery in remission from his opium addiction. Initial reactions to *The Hound of Heaven* proved cautiously enthusiastic. But when, three years later, now more widely available in Thompson's first volume of published poetry, it famously took the critics by storm. Today, translated into more than sixty languages, everything from Afrikaans to Zulu, it has become one of only a handful of English religious poems to appeal to all nationalities and faiths. While it certainly remains his most famous poem, but is it his best?

This enduring poetic rhapsody, one hundred and eighty two lines long, represents the writer's most ambitious and, for many, most successful achievement. Here he was able to fuse together a language of striking originality with an intense emotional force. Moments of great power sit alongside, and seamlessly integrate with more lyrical passages. Long the subject of countless articles, analyses, dramas and documentaries, the poem has proved no less inspirational to artists, writers and musicians. It is not, after all, a repentance for iniquity, so much as a statement of the incompleteness of earthly human satisfaction. While for some it remains an acquired taste, for countless others, once acquired it undoubtedly lodges obstinately in the memory.

One critic famously described the poem as a second Gerontius - a generous tribute to its power and its somewhat intense passionate sincerity. Here Thompson comes to us as the Bard, claiming to reveal that his vision of the Kingdom of God is not to be found, *in no strange land*, but all around us. Though totally humble himself, Thompson never doubted the validity of his beliefs. Such unshakeable confidence ultimately brings an exhilarating quality to the work, adding a speed and urgency, so rarely found in poetry of this period. And yet doubts occasionally surface, particularly with regard to the extent Thompson succeeded in adequately embodying his vision in words. Was he truly a religious seer, or, as many have suggested, merely a neurotic dreamer?[2]

Here we have a single great theme and a clear progression of feeling to give unity to the whole. It details man's attempt to escape from God, who is portrayed as this relentless omniscient and omnipresent Hound. Written entirely in the first person, it opens by thrusting the reader into the chase. While the symbols and images suggested by Thompson's own religious worship have a special appeal to the Catholic minded reader, they have never stood in the way of the work's more general acceptance. Many have detected numerous influences within the poem, its inner coherence helped by the likes of Blake, Keats, Byron, Tennyson, Wordsworth, Shelley, Herbert and Swinburne, together with the talents of Isaiah, St John and, not least, the myriad authors of *The Psalms*.

The Hound of Heaven also played an important role in the development of many of those who followed in the poet's wake. Both Robert Frost and Eugene O'Neill, during their apprentice days, benefitted from its craftsmanship. Frost, a Pulitzer Prize winner, writing in the *Boston Globe* in 1957, recalled his first contact with the work in a local book store. Forced to use his bus fare to purchase the poem, he was then left with no option but to walk home. Having learnt the work by heart, Eugene O'Neill, a Nobel Laureate in Literature, was forever quoting it complete to anyone who would listen. Worldwide attention duly came its way in 1954, when one of its many effective phrases-*deliberate speed*-famously turned up in a landmark case in America's Supreme Court about segregation.

The novelist, Graham Greene made good use of another of its oft-quoted lines when he called one of his finest novels, *The Labyrinthine Ways.*[3] For the American market this later became *The Power and the Glory.* A.J. Cronin, he of *The Citadel* fame, uses the poem in his novel, *A Pocketful of Rye*[4], as does Daphne du Maurier in *Rebecca.*[5] Not to be outdone, it also makes an appearance in one of Colin Dexter's Inspector Morse stories, *The Last Enemy.*[6] In 1933, Halliday Sutherland's best-selling autobiography was entitled *The Arches of the Years*[7], while Hollywood actor, Dean Jones, titled his autobiography, *Under Running Laughter.*[8] Constantly battling extreme depression, while starring in countless hugely-popular Disney movies, and forever haunted by the poem, Jones related how faith not fame eventually changed his life for the better.

In 1914, a then little-known artist, Frideswith Huddart became one of the first to illustrate Francis Thompson's poetry.[9] A daughter of the manse, born in Yorkshire in 1881, Caroline Sophia Frideswith Huddart would later go on to study at Regent Street Polytechnic and exhibit regularly in London. Marrying a Dutch nobleman, Count Robert van Lynden, who became the Liberian Ambassador to London, her later output included an illustrated companion to *The Psalms.* She died in London in 1964. Another who took the visual content of Thompson's poem as a basis for her designs, was the English illustrator, Jean Young.[10] Likewise, the American artist, Robert Hale Ives Gammell, whose numerous paintings also attempt to unite the many religious, mythical and psychological inherent strands within the work.[11]

In 1954, the prolific and highly accomplished Polish-American sculptor, Theodore Roszak, finally got round to creating his own intensely personal take on *The Hound of Heaven.* Born in 1907, the year Francis Thompson died, Roszak is perhaps best known for his 37 foot gilded aluminium eagle, sited on the pediment of the former American Embassy building in London's Grosvenor Square, that was installed in 1960. Much smaller, though still some 6ft tall, Roszak's personal vision of the poem, having taken some years to come to fruition, is strikingly constructed, built mainly in steel, together with distinctive infusions of nickel-silver and copper. It is now one of many prized exhibits housed in the Museum of Modern Art in New York, a gift from his estate, following the sculptor's death in 1981.

Some years earlier during the course of 1936, 1,200 young people, members of the Roman Catholic Youth Organisation, known as the Society of the Grail put on a mimed dramatization of *The Hound of Heaven*, set amid the grandeur of the Royal Albert Hall.[12] Everybody connected with one private and the three public performances, from costume and scenery designers to actors and musicians, remained anonymous. With backing from the mighty organ and two pianos, the music incorporates everything from Palestrina, Plainsong, Mozart and Elgar, while extracts from the Bible, both chanted and sung, were interpolated with the music of J.S. Bach. In 1968, *The Laurel and The Poppy*, a stage play based on the poem by Margaret Gillett and Monica Kehoe opened in London's West End.

Large scale musical settings of the text were pioneered by a then little known English composer, William Harris. The son of a postal official, born in London in 1883, William Henry Harris began his illustrious career as a choir boy at St James Church, Tulse Hill. While at school he held several appointments at local churches. He then became an articled pupil of Herbert Morris at the somewhat remote cathedral at St David's in West Wales. In 1899, he emerged from this time-honoured apprenticeship to become one of the youngest Fellows of the Royal College of Organists ever to pass their examinations. Winning the Lord Charles Bruce Organ Scholarship to study at the Royal College of Music, there his career was guided by Charles Wood, Henry Walford Davies, and Sir Walter Parratt.

In 1911, while Assistant Organist to John Lott at Lichfield Cathedral, he taught at the Birmingham and Midland Institute, working under the guidance of Sir Granville Bantock. With his early compositional career at this time showing real flair and inspiration, it remains questionable what he might have achieved had he remained close to Bantock instead of maintaining an almost monastic devotion to the daily offices of the Church of England at New College, Christ Church, and St George's Chapel Windsor. While there, from 1933 until retirement in 1961, he also served as a Professor at the Royal College of Music, and was, for a time, Director of Studies at the Royal School of Church Music. He also taught two young princesses, Elizabeth and Margaret, to play the piano. He was knighted in 1954.

Throughout his long and distinguished career, Harris completed a considerable output of well-written music, always effective and well adapted to the needs of the people it was meant to serve. While at Windsor he became something of a composer-laureate, producing works for royal and state occasions. These include, *O Hearken Thou*, written for the 1937 Coronation and, for the 1953 service, *Let My Prayer Come Up*. Music on a more expansive and personally distinctive canvas includes the fine *Song on May Morning* alongside the unaccompanied double choir anthems, *Faire Is The Heaven* and *Bring Us, O Lord, At Our Last Awakening*. During the 1939-45 War his instrumental music was also heard at the Sir Henry Wood Promenade Concerts, Harris himself doing the conducting.

A quarter of a century earlier, after serving with the 28th London Regiment in the First World War, Harris returned to Lichfield to begin work on his first major choral piece, a challenging setting for Baritone, Chorus and Orchestra of Francis Thompson's *The Hound of Heaven*. Described as a Fantasy by the composer, Harris sets the complete poem save for seven lines. The work runs without a break. In 1919, it was awarded a coveted prize in the prestigious Carnegie United Kingdom Trust Publication Scheme. The adjudicators report was as follows: *"It successfully solves a difficult problem in its adaptability to the restless moods of the poem. The various episodes are distinguished by a well-defined character, and the music rises to an exalted expression at the close."*

First performed on 4th December 1918, at Birmingham Town Hall, with his colleague from the Birmingham and Midland Institute, Allen Blackall, conducting the Birmingham Festival Chorus and Orchestra, Robert Parker was the Baritone soloist. Also on the programme was the Coronation Scene from *Boris Godonov* by Mussorgsky, the second act of Gluck's *Orpheus* and the Choral Dances from *Prince Igor*. Positive reviews prompted a repeat performance the following season, again with Allen Blackall in charge, though this time with Captain Horace Stevens the vocal soloist. Eighteen months later, under the auspices of the South Staffordshire Musical Festival, the work was performed in Walsall by the local Philharmonic Society and the City of Birmingham Orchestra.

The work is scored for:

Flute	Two Horns
Piccolo	Trumpet
Oboe	Trombone
Cor Anglaise	Timpani
Clarinets	Harp
Bassoon	Organ
Strings	

Constructed rather freely within six major sections, Harris's magnum opus opens with a sombre orchestral introduction in G minor. After three bars of quiet sustained chords, the French Horns introduce one of the major motifs which, in typical Wagnerian fashion, the composer cleverly transforms as the work slowly unfolds. Passing from *Lento*, through *Animato* before settling into *Allegro Moderato*, this opening theme is cleverly expanded amid an increasingly rich chromatic panoply. Then the poem begins, at first sung by the choral basses in a simple statement on a repeated note before being taken up by the tenors. Adding urgency, over a rich orchestral texture, is the baritone soloist, before a somewhat ill-defined key structure brings yet further impetus.

As the choir sing in unison the words, *But with unhurrying chase*, here as elsewhere in the work, the listener is transported back to the world of ancient plainsong, though now in twentieth century garb. Likewise, Harris's use of rapidly changing time signatures, triplet figurations and the frequent imposition of *hemiola*, this the superimposing of two notes in the time of three, or three in the time of two. Offering contrast and moments of repose is the divided unaccompanied choral writing at the line, *Fear wist not to evade as Love wist to pursue.* A shortened version of the middle section of the opening instrumental introduction brings the listener to the next major section which allows the baritone soloist an opportunity to flex his vocal chords, amid a judicious mix of recitative and aria.

It is at this point that the composer now chooses to introduce an important new theme within the orchestral texture. Set firmly in the key of B flat major, over tonic and dominant harmonies, despite many later transformations, its upward sweep remains increasingly apparent. Following some gentle imitative writing for the choral forces, a delightful interplay between choir and soloist moves effortlessly through numerous key changes. A pause and a change of key from the richness of A flat major to the rather plainer F major heralds the apex of the work. This central adagio section, initially unaccompanied, is dominated by the baritone soloist. Here again, the composer judiciously mixes aria and recitative, the vocal writing exploring the full extent of the singer's range.

Nigh and nigh draws the chase, intone the choir quietly in unison, before the music builds to a climax at the words, *Naked I wait Thy love's uplifted stroke!* The intensity and momentum heighten, aided by a thickening of orchestral textures and chromatic decorations that seem to fly in the face of the stated key signature. Coming towards the end is an unaccompanied divisi choral passage, sung pp to the words, *Strange piteous futile thing.* Marked to be performed with the utmost freedom, it remains one of the many high points of the work. Gradually re-joined by the orchestra, there is just time for the soloist to interject before the choir, now in G major and in seven part harmony, move the work to a sublime conclusion, gently intoning, *I am He who thou seekest.*

As one of the winners of that prestigious 1919 Carnegie Award[13], William Harris should have been anticipating many regular performances and extensive sales for his composition. However, delays in publication meant that the work sadly never fully established itself. Instead, it was overshadowed by another of the winners, Gustav Holst's, *Hymn of Jesus*, a composer who himself had already come to set Francis Thompson's poetry to music.[14] Performed in Rochester once more in 1948, *The Hound of Heaven* was recently revived by the conductor, Paul Spicer. He would later write: *This was a real voyage of discovery-and what a real sense of anticipation towards what felt like a world premiere performance. It lasts an hour and encompasses a world of emotions, moods and choral textures.*[15]

It was again in Birmingham Town Hall some thirty six years later, on 16th November 1954, that another extensive setting of *The Hound of Heaven* also had its premiere. On that particular occasion, the City of Birmingham Choir and Symphony Orchestra were guided by David Willcocks. This time the composer was Maurice Jacobson.[16] Born in London on 1 January 1897, his prodigious musical talents were first nurtured as a piano scholar at the Modern School of Music in London where he was taught by the distinguished Italian pianist, Ferruccio Busoni. Winning an open scholarship to the Royal College of Music in 1916, amid a break for military service during the First World War, he then studied with Charles Villiers Stanford, Gustav Holst and Adrian Boult.

Although from a Jewish family, Jacobson never considered himself a Jewish composer. For many years he served as Choirmaster at the West London Synagogue in Upper Brook Street, the headquarters of Reform Judaism in Britain. In addition, an adjudicator of world renown, it was when officiating at the 1937 Carlisle Festival, that he first came across a then unknown contralto, Kathleen Ferrier. Over the years, he would later prove an invaluable mentor, helping guide her all too short career. While a regular broadcaster for the BBC, in 1923 Jacobson joined the music publishing firm of J. Curwen and Sons, initially as a music editor. Having played a key role in ensuring the company's survival throughout the Second World War, from 1950 until 1972, he served as Company Chairman.

Amid all these many and varied roles, Jacobson remained a prolific and popular composer with music in all forms flowing from his pen. Here orchestral works, piano solos and duets, incidental music and ballet suites sit alongside notable choral works such as *The Lady of Shalott*. A long-time admirer of Francis Thompson's poem, Jacobson scored his setting of *The Hound of Heaven* for Tenor Solo, Choir and an Orchestra, comprising triple woodwind, four horns, three trumpets, three trombones, tuba, timpani, percussion, harp and strings. Following its premiere, subsequent performances included an Easter Sunday broadcast in the United States, another in New Zealand and one here, on 2 January 1976, in honour of the composer's 80th birthday, exactly a month before his death.

Marked *Molto Lento*, the work opens with four solemn chords in the strings over a held pedal G. Somewhat archaic in nature, courtesy of their modal flattened sevenths and used as a unifying device, they are repeated at various points throughout the work. After this short introduction, the choir then enters softly in unison, intoning the text, *I fled Him, down the arches of the years*, in a rhythmical chant somewhat reminiscent of plainsong. The avoidance of strong accents adds to the feeling of restlessness. As the unison opens out briefly to harmony, the first section ends at the words, *All things betray thee, who betrayest Me*. Sopranos and altos now combine against tenors and basses, over an orchestral double pedal, while a high B on a solo violin emphasises the tonality.

A change to triple time brings the first appearance of the tenor soloist as both texture and atmosphere intensify. A recall of the opening orchestral chords and the earlier music of, *All things betray thee*, but now sung to the words, *Naught shelters thee, who wilt not shelter Me*. A change of key to D flat major adds further colour to the writing. Here, an increasingly unaccompanied soloist and chorus interact in a most delightful way. The divisi vocal melismas on *Wantoning*, are especially moving, as is a later section where a wordless chorus on *Ah*, adds a wonderfully ethereal atmosphere. Contrast comes in the form of the succeeding choral passage, a fluid but challenging, somewhat abstract, fugato section, centred around the key of E major.

The orchestra seamlessly moves the key back to D flat major as the tenor soloist re-enters with a technically demanding vocal line that encompasses a number of high B flats. The orchestral transition repeats earlier material before a luminous instrumental texture of high solo violin harmonics, string tremolando, repeated woodwind chords, sustained horns and timpani, subtly underpins a choral section beginning with the words, *Nigh and nigh draws the chase*. All this is vividly linked by the recurring opening motif. Here as elsewhere, imaginative accompanimental textures and colours are very much in evidence, and while the orchestration itself was never intended to be a major feature, the composer's debt to his great hero, Maurice Ravel, is evident on every page.

The crucial words of the Hound, *And is thy earth so marr'd*, are given to the unaccompanied chorus before the opening instrumental chords return in their original key. The music is at this point very pastoral in nature, as one by one the choral voices enter. Here, with the tenor soloist sensing his final enlightenment, the music rises to an intense orchestral climax. All that remains is for the chorus, divided into eight part textures and their notation values doubled, to respond in kind. A high tremolo G in the violins can be heard as the words, *I am He*, moves gently through the two choirs. As the instruments gradually drop out, all that is left are the soprano voices in choir 1 on a major third, supported by a violin tremolando G. Both that and the voices fade gently into the distance.

While Maurice Jacobson was only a year older than the Norwegian composer, Fartein Valen, there remained a huge gulf of difference over their musical outlook. A pupil of Elling at the Copenhagen Conservatoire of Music and then Max Bruch at the Berlin Musikhockschule, Valen developed a highly personal twelve note style, richly polyphonic, but at the same time, also clear and lyrical. Among his extensive output, the three movement atonal odyssey that is the *Second Piano Sonata*, is directly inspired by *The Hound of Heaven*. No less influenced was popular English singer and composer, Kate Bush, whose second song on her fifth album, *Hounds of Love*, recorded in 1985, tells of the obsessive pursuit from which the singer runs.[17] As someone searching for a way to escape, here yet again it seemingly takes its lead from Thompson's poem.

Music critic, Stanley Webb, also got it absolutely right when, in 1971, reviewing Noel Rawsthorne's magisterial recording of a number of famous toccatas, played on the enormous Willis organ in Liverpool's Anglican Cathedral, he wrote: *Francis Thompson's line-deliberate speed, majestic instancy-springs to mind as one by one these familiar show pieces roll sonorously off the disc and the wonderful Willis pipework speaks out in all its glory.*[18] That same year, again with *The Hound of Heaven* as his inspiration, Malcolm Williamson wrote *Peace Pieces for Organ* to perform on his inaugural American tour.[19] As a Roman Catholic convert himself, he had earlier created a hugely-challenging, *Symphony for Organ*, for Allan Wicks, at that time the Organist of Canterbury Cathedral, the poetic impulse of its fifth movement, a Passacaglia, entitled *Aria II*, once again directly relates to Thompson's poem.

Another composer long in awe of Thompson's poetry is Howard Blake. Born in London in 1938, he studied with Harold Craxton and Howard Ferguson at the Royal Academy of Music. A rarity on the contemporary music scene, being a genuinely popular composer, he is perhaps best known for the success of *The Snowman*. Adapted from a story by Raymond Briggs, particularly memorable is its haunting theme tune, *Walking in the Air*. His extensive output also includes music for film and television. More extended choral works include *The Song of Saint Francis*, a cantata for SATB chorus and orchestra, *Stabat Mater*, an oratorio for soprano, treble, tenor bass, SATB chorus and orchestra, *The Bells*, a cantata for SA chorus and orchestra and a large-scale setting, entitled *Benedictus*. Commissioned by the Ditchling Choral Society, this was first performed in Worth Abbey in Sussex, on 10 May 1980.

Divided into three sections, in Part 1 of *Benedictus*, the Novice's despair is countered by affirmations of faith. In Part 2 the chorus declares the disciplines required to enter monastic life, the Novice then examines his innermost soul in words from *The Hound of Heaven*, set mainly for tenor soloist. A briefly glimpsed vision of spiritual ecstasy leads to Part 3, the ritual of admission to the Order and a joyous psalm of blessing. St Benedict's own words from The Rule of St Benedict are articulated by the Speaker at key moments along this journey. Lasting some 70 minutes, the work is scored for tenor, speaker, chorus, solo viola and orchestra.[20] A setting of another Thompson poem. *The Kingdom of God*, has long been proposed by the composer, though sadly, the opportunity has not yet arisen.

Among the younger generation of composers attracted by the poet's colourful word play and inventive vocabulary is the cleric, conductor and composer, Ronald Corp. Born in Wells in 1951, after reading Music at Christ Church, Oxford, while also serving as an Anglican Priest, he has combined numerous musical activities, both here and abroad. Having initially established his reputation with Finchley Children's Group, in 1988 he founded the New London Orchestra, adding the New London Children's Choir, three years later. In 1987, he distilled his extensive knowledge into what has become a seminal text, *The Choral Singer's Companion*. Chairman of the Musicians Benevolent Fund, for this and his many other charitable endeavours, in 2012, he received the O.B.E.

Despite having destroyed most of his early works, today Corp's compositional output remains both extensive and wide-ranging. Heading the list are a large number of diverse choral cantatas. These include *And All the Trumpets Sounded*, *Laudamus*, *A New Song*, *Mary's Song*, *Adonai* and *The Waters of Time*. Premiered in Wells Cathedral by the BBC Singers and 240 local school children in 2006, it celebrates the history and people of Sedgemoor and the Mendip areas of his native Somerset. *Dover Beach* was commissioned in 2006 by the BBC Singers while, in the same year, *This Sceptr'd Isle*, honoured Queen Elizabeth II's sixty year reign. A fine *Piano Concerto* dates from 1997, while an impressive *Symphony* followed ten years later, together with a challenging *String Quartet*.

Having previously set a number of Francis Thompson poems in a song cycle for counter tenor and piano, in 2009, Corp was asked by a member of the New London Chorus to compose a setting of *The Hound of Heaven*. First performed by The London Chorus and the New London Orchestra, this twenty five minute work for S.A.T.B. Choir and Orchestra was given its premiere at the Cadogan Hall later that year. It is scored for:

Three Flutes	Three Trombones
Two Oboes	One Tuba
Two Clarinets	Timpani
Four Horns	Harp
Two Trumpets	Strings

The whole poem is set, sung without a break and subdivided into four main sections. Responding brilliantly to the text, a syncopated repeated tonic dominant bass figure alongside a descending triplet motif in the accompaniment, adds momentum to a descending dotted vocal line. Initially strophic in design, a baritone soloist then takes over before the opening thematic ideas are very effectively recalled. The second section, now in gentle triple time and beginning with the words, *I sought no more after which I strayed In face of man or maid*, uses a lyrical orchestral motif to break-up the vocal harmony. A change to the minor key brings in the baritone soloist, before a tierce de Picardie heralds a beautifully judged solo for a soprano who begins, *Come then, Ye other Children.*

Fast approaching is the heart of Corp's work, marked Allegro Scherzo, and in compound triple time, where high voices are continually echoed by lower. Brief imitative motifs all add to the intensity, before the tension is quickly defused with an orchestral diminuendo. A move to E flat major brings back the baritone soloist, *Naked I wait the love's uplifted stroke!* before the chorus then take over. The fourth and final section recalls fragments from the opening. Here other themes are cleverly re-introduced as the work builds to a climax. The brief use of the lyrical second subject accompanying the baritone soloist, *Halts by me that footfall*, allows the choir to respond gently. A final recall of the tonic dominant orchestral motif from the very opening brings about a lasting unity.

Since Gabriel's 'Blessed Damozel' no mystical words have so touched me as The Hound of Heaven, wrote the celebrated artist, Edward Burne-Jones in 1894.[21] Fifty years later, at the height of the Second World War, the distinguished and highly-decorated soldier, Field Marshall Viscount Wavell expressed similar sentiments in the introduction to his anthology of poetry, *Other Men's Flowers*:

> The Hound of Heaven has had a special place in my life, as a charm in danger or trouble. Many years ago, a friend gave me a copy of Francis Thompson's lyric at St. Andrews, where I was playing golf. I had it by heart in a very few readings and from that day I have used the magic of its imagery in my times

> of stress, to distract my mind from peril or disaster. I have repeated the words of this greatest of all lyrics under fire, on a rough Channel crossing, in pain of body or mind.[22]

To celebrate the 75th anniversary of the creation of the work, a commemorative exhibition, complete with a detailed catalogue was organised to take place in London, appropriately at 47 Palace Court. Somewhat later than initially planned, it eventually took place on 21st January 1967. Organised by The Francis Thompson Society under the auspices of its founder, the Indian born academic, Dr Gutala Krishnamurti, it was opened amid much pomp and ceremony by the Deputy Mayor of Westminster. The chief guest was the poet's eminent godson, Sir Francis Meynell, the main speaker being the President of the Society, the author, Henry Williamson, while the poem was read by the distinguished actor, Marius Goring. As was widely reported at the time, this rather unusual event brought enthusiastic letters of support from, among others, the Pope, the Dalai Lama and the Hindu religious leader, his Holiness Jagadgura Shenkaracharya Maharaj.

In sending their best wishes for the success of the event, Pope Paul talked of the poem's spiritual and moral influence, the Dalai Lama referred to the importance of poetry in man's search for aesthetic ideals while the Hindu leader claimed that Thompson was a great mystic, " in direct contact with the Reality." For Henry Williamson, it remained one of the shortest autobiographies in English or any other language. It was an evolutionary poem of the clearest truth, remaining unique yet universal. He duly went on to remind everyone present that, *The Hound of Heaven* was not the only great poem that Thompson ever wrote. Anyone who took the time and trouble to explore the many other lesser known aspects of Thompson's work would surely be no less inspired by what they would find.

Chapter 5

POETRY AND PROSE

> It is perfectly safe to affirm that if Mr Thompson wrote no other line, by this volume alone he is as secure of remembrance as any poet of the century. Such a volume of poetry has not appeared in Queen Victoria's time more authentic in utterance than this.

The eminent critic of the time, James Garvin, writing in *The Newcastle Daily Chronicle* and enthusiastically endorsing the quality of Francis Thompson's first published volume of poetry, which appeared to universal acclaim in 1893[1]. Dedicated to Wilfrid and Alice Meynell, it was this collection that so spectacularly launched the poet on to the literary landscape. Looking back, it now seems somewhat surprising, given his intense personal history of suffering and addiction, that not one of his poems, except perhaps *Dream Tryst*, was written with the assistance of opium. Of his three major collections, *Poems* (1893) and *Sister Songs* (1895) were created during his time at Storrington, while *New Poems* followed two years later. By then, he was in the care of the Capuchin Friars in North Wales.

It was late in May, 1893, when Francis Thompson first received news that the publisher, John Lane, had enquired about producing a volume of his poetry. For this Meynell submitted assorted examples of Thompson's earlier work, previously published in *Merry England*. With the publishers subsequently reporting back most enthusiastically, by June of that year, the poet was hard at work preparing the final manuscript. Here he brought together a collection of texts he had written earlier for Alice Meynell, selecting a further eleven pieces for rigorous revision. From July onwards, he focussed purely on proof reading, prior to eventual publication in November, 1893.

Simply entitled *Poems* and published by the Bodley Head Publishing House, its impact was immediate. Eighty pages in length, the volume was highly unusual in having a somewhat square old-fashioned format. Each poem was well placed and spaced on thick art paper, the grey/green covers bearing a simple but highly effective design of gold circles. The frontispiece, designed by a then unknown poet, Laurence Housman, who had recently provided illustrations for collections by John Davidson and Katharine Tynan, visualised the "hearted casement" passage in *The Hound of Heaven*. For the poet himself, it proved a step too far.

In view of everything that had passed in the intervening years, it is perhaps no surprise that the volume opens with a Dedication:

To Wilfrid and Alice Meynell

If the rose in meek duty
May dedicate humbly
To her grower the beauty
Wherewith she is comely,
If the mine to the miner
The jewels that pined in it,
Earth to diviner
The springs he divined in it,
To the grapes the wine-pitcher
Their juice that was crushed in it,
Viol to its witcher
The music lay hushed in it,
If the lips may pay Gladness
In laughters she wakened,
And the heart to its sadness
Weeping unslakened,
If the hid and sealed coffer,
Whose having not his is,
To the loosers may proffer
Their finding-here this is;
Their lives if all livers
To the Life of all living,
To you, O dear givers!
I give your own giving.

Comprising eighteen separate works and essentially tripartite in overall design, this first volume can easily be subdivided into three major titled sections: *Love in Dian's Lap*; a middle collection which Thompson labelled

Miscellaneous Poems, with *The Hound of Heaven* at its core; before closing with a series of *Poems on Children*. Undoubtedly inspired by the poet's enduring reverence for Alice Meynell, *Love in Dian's Lap* comprises a series of seven odes which, while undoubtedly showing influences of Shelley and Patmore, explore various aspects of love, be it mystical or platonic. Beginning in August, 1890 and compiled over a period of three years, though somewhat uncharacteristic of his output up to this date, nevertheless it is his enduring passion for language that shines through most strongly.

Despite Thompson's dislike of writing verse to order, in January 1892, following the death of Cardinal Manning and a request from Wilfrid Meynell, he very quickly produced the memorable *To the Dead Cardinal of Westminster*. Opening the middle section of the volume, this work had first appeared in the February edition of *Merry England*, Thompson having, most unusually, completed the forty four carefully crafted stanzas within the space three or four days. Here, sharing a personal knowledge and interest in the subject, the short lines and brief stanzas, achieve a most moving impetus. For many, however, the work has little to do with the subject itself, but much more to do with Thompson's own continuing sense of inadequacy.

The Hound of Heaven, which becomes the major focus of the *Miscellaneous* section of the volume, while not entirely free from the occasional disfiguring qualities of the love odes, nevertheless its strength of original thought and execution place it on an altogether higher plain. It has a universality that allows it to appeal to many who have no interest at all in poetry or even religion. Its main theme, the pursuit of the soul by God, is derived by the poet from *The Confessions of St Augustine*. Thus, within his central poetic purpose, Thompson is able to bring a semblance of control to his verbal virtuosity. Sadly, in the little known, *A Corymbus for Autumn*, such discipline is all too rarely apparent.

A corymb or corymbus is the botanical term for a cluster of flowers in which the individual flowers form a flat or slightly convex head, as in scabious or Ivy flowers. To produce this shape, it is evident that the further the flowers are from the centre, the longer their stems must be. Here, as in Thompson's *A Corymbus for Autumn*, each of the succeeding stanzas gets longer. It was a model that the English composer, Edmund Rubbra, adopted within the first movement of his elegant, but sadly neglected *Piano Concerto in G major.*[2] Each of the two main musical themes is expanded every time they appear. In addition, they also become freer, while two features, repeated notes in the second and fourth bars and a two-against-three rhythm, constantly recall the work's original theme.

Amid a constant sense of guilt over his opiate addiction, Thompson also had a long and tortuous struggle with the often vexed question of religious conviction versus artistic freedom. Exploring this dilemma in some highly personal detail was *A Judgement in Heaven*, written in the summer of 1892 and, like numerous other works in the collection, first published in *Merry England.* Here the Poet is clearly a reflection of Thompson himself. In what was yet another long and extensive offering, *Mary Magdalen* calls attention to the poet's travails who, when stripped of all dishonest thoughts, is merely seen as a poor and sinful figure. While his poetic powers are viewed as the gift of God, thanks to the constant pain he suffered when cursed by the divine gift of poetry, his sins are subsequently forgiven.

In contrast, within the refreshing simplicity of *Epilogue*, Thompson is again much exercised by the question of the relationship between a poet's character as a man and the quality of his verse. It was a theme he had previously explored within an article on Shelley which had been published in *Merry England* in September, 1892. For Thompson, Shelley was one whose idealistic sufferings as an artist might well be thought of as a penalty for the sins of his life. Indeed, the central figure of the poem, the Poet, again might well be Thompson himself. In common with *A Fallen Yew, A Judgement in Heaven*, shows the poet fast approaching a maturity, able to express a highly individual vision that falls just tantalisingly short of his most accomplished artistry.

Beginning with *Daisy*, the five *Poems on Children* which bring this first collection to a conclusion, perhaps form the poet's least ambitious but, for many, his most effective achievement so far. Of all the Meynell children it was Monica whose character appealed to him the most. During the summer of 1891, while holidaying with the family at Friston in Suffolk, she pulled a flower from the grass and instinctively gave it to him. While forming the inspiration for *The Poppy*, the opium flower proved a poignant reminder of the poet's own misspent youth. In May of 1891, another child, a boy, was born to Wilfrid and Alice. Named Francis in his honour, Thompson was delighted to become his godfather. Within a few days the family had received a new offering from the poet entitled, *To My Godchild.*

This first volume of poetry ends with perhaps one of his most moving works addressed very directly to the Meynell children, *To Monica Thought Dying.* Early in 1892, the whole family attended Cardinal Manning's lengthy funeral obsequies, which took place amid bitter winter weather. As a result, daughter Monica developed pleurisy and for several days her life was in danger. After taking delight in the child's early play in her toy shop, where she distributed sweets to all who would buy, Thompson changes the mood in a most mature and dramatic fashion. Cleverly using the example of Coventry Patmore's *If I Were Dead*, such is the power and intensity of *Monica Thought Dying* that the reader is able to hear the plaintive cries of someone sobbing in the night.

Following the publication of *Poems*, Thompson was hailed by some as a great visionary poet. However, as has always been the case, the reaction to his poetry has often been mixed. While Arnold Bennett declared that Thompson was only excelled in natural genius by William Shakespeare[3], in contrast, Clement Shorter, while a member of the Meynell inner circle, thought Francis Thompson was nothing more than "a small Catholic poet."[4] In an age of Oscar Wilde, there was undoubtedly a great deal of interest in Thompson's somewhat bohemian background, not least his long period spent in often total seclusion, amid the isolation of monastic life. While Wilfrid Meynell revelled in his protégé's success, as for Thompson himself, his view of his new found status was often less than joyful.

Surprisingly perhaps one of the most balanced yet penetrating reviews of this first volume appeared in *The Fortnightly Review*. Its author was Coventry Patmore, who had himself lent a hand in preparing the poems for publication. Save for Patmore's somewhat slavish devotion to Alice Meynell, he praises Thompson's verse as equal to Crashaw and finds special interest in the poet's handling of the irregular ode form. He also singles out *The Hound of Heaven* for special praise, notwithstanding the occasional defects of language. The work particularly appealed to him because it explored the hitherto almost unworked mine of Catholic philosophy, its spirituality giving evidence of the real ardour of life, and not its mere negation.

Having quickly moved through three editions in the first three months following its initial publication, this first volume very quickly earned royalties well in excess of £100. For Meynell, as keeper of the purse, it represented the first of many large financial returns he would garner from the poet's work over the course of the next half century. Keen to capitalize on the interest and excitement engendered by the success of this first collection, Meynell urged a somewhat reluctant poet to build on the momentum and seize such an opportunity with a further volume. The work chosen for this second publication was *Sister Songs*. Thus, in December 1894, Thompson returned to London to spend Christmas and the New Year working on the finished manuscript.

As events turned out Thompson's initial reluctance to publish would prove well founded. First appearing in print in June 1895, at more than one thousand lines in length, *Sister Songs*, proved a huge disappointment both among readers and critics alike. It sold a mere five hundred and ninety nine copies in its first six months. Originally entitled *Amphicypellon*, the name of an ancient two handed cup, its title again recalls Shelley, as indeed does the overall nature of the work itself. When Meynell insisted on changing this, Thompson compromised by retaining his subtitle, *An Offering to Two Sisters*. They are of course, the two Meynell girls, the first part addressed to Madeline, using her family name of Sylvia, the second to Monica, the elder of the two;

> Love and love's beauty only hold their revels
> In life's familiar, penetrable levels:
> What of its ocean floor?
> I dwell there evermore.
> From almost earlies youth
> I raised the lids o' the truth,
> And forced her bend on me her shrinking sight;
> Ever I knew me Beauty's eremite,
> In antre of this lowly body set,
> Girt with a thirsty solitude of soul.

Critic and poet, Professor Edward Dowden surely spoke for many when, reviewing *Sister Songs*, he offered the poet some salutary advice in *The Illustrated London News* of 10th August, 1895:

> At various periods in the history of literature there have been some poets, possessing admirable gifts of ardour, imagination, fancy, melodious utterance, who have not served their art wholly well. They have created beauty, and they have marred their own creation. They have carved statues, and not content with what was well done, have proceeded to tattoo their statues. It is to be feared the Mr Thompson will be remembered among these. No one who has a feeling for poetry can question that he is essentially that rare thing, a poet; no one who knows the difference between right and wrong can help perceiving that he often abuses his remarkable powers. We find so much to admire that we are ready to forgive; But in art it does not lie with any of us to pronounce a pardon; the offender must bear his own offence. If the writer cannot pursue a high theme without being diverted to chase every butterfly conceit that flits across his path, it means that passion or imagination with him are intermittent; if his fancies are sometimes ingenious and no more, it means that surprise attracts him more than beauty; if his diction be overloaded with exotic curiosities, it means that, while seeking virtuosity, he has not attained mastery of his instrument; if he should catch at petty decorations of verse, it means that his is lacking in artistic continence. And has imperfect sense of relative values. Mr Thompson is assuredly a poet; he has it in him to be an eminent poet in his own order, as a writer of the lyric, not the lyric of direct passion, but of imaginative

> exultation. If, however, he refuses to admit that his artistic sins are sinful, if he persists in calling evil good, he cannot surpass his present self; he will probably give us some short poems of extraordinary excellence, and a waste of verse in which blossoms of beauty will ever grow more rare and weeds more rampant. No critic can save a poet from the vice of artistic incontinence; but a poet may before it is too late, endeavour to deliver his better self from its snares and temptations........
>
> Mr Thompson's exotic vocabulary is no improvement on the tongue that Shakespeare spake. If a novelty of diction be imported it should, it should be done discreetly, and a place should be found for it. The words of the lexicon should not be used to pelt our ears, like decorative brickbats. Shakespeare speaks of blood that incarnadines the multitudinous seas, but he does not add, "making the virid sole sanguine"; he prefers "making the green one red."
>
> No one is likely to esteem more highly Mr Thompson's rare gifts as a poet than the writer of this article; but time, which reserved the judgment of critics, is not on the side of absurdity.

For one Thompson biographer, Rodolphe Louis Mégroz, writing a little over twenty years later, just after the poet's death, *Sister Songs*, "contains the finest metaphysical poetry of nature ever written in English until Thompson himself produced still finer."[5] Few among even the most ardent admirers of Thompson's work would surely nowadays agree with such effusive praise. And yet, there is still much to be admired within the poetry, not least the poet's genuine love of children but, above all, their innocence. But what of the two young Meynell girls, Madeline and Monica, who so inspired the work? "We were utterly bored by it all," they invariably responded.[6]

However, the critical hostility towards *Sister Songs* did little to dampen his publisher's enthusiasm in general for Thompson's work. Invited to provide a further third poetry collection, he undertook an extensive period of creativity that would occupy him throughout the latter part of 1895 and well into 1896. On completion, he wrote:

> This book represents the work of the three years which have elapsed since my first volume was prepared for the press, my second volume having been a poem of comparatively early date. The first section exhibits mysticism in a limited and varying degree. I feel my instrument yet too imperfect to profane by it the higher ranges. Much is transcendental rather than truly mystic.[7]

To the above Thompson also added:

> Of words I have coined or revived I have seen fit to retain but few; and not more than two or three will be found in this book. I shall also be found, I hope, to have modified much the excessive loading both of diction and imagery which disfigured my former work.[8]

Despite what seems to be an increasing sense of self criticism, one noted academic found that out of one hundred and eighty three rare, archaic or obsolete words so beloved by Thompson, a whole eighty eight appear in this new volume. In addition, of some one hundred and thirty four words specifically created by the poet, seventy six also relate to this same volume.

Published by Constable in 1897, this third and final volume of some fifty three works, was simply titled, *New Poems*. Here Thompson now meticulously sub-divides his output into four major sections; *Sight and Insight*; *A Narrow Vessel*; *Miscellaneous Odes*; and *Ultima*. This particular collection opens with a dedication to his friend and fellow poet, Coventry Patmore, whose influence undoubtedly pervades the whole enterprise. Tragically, Patmore died[9] before the volume appeared in print, Thompson then adding the following to his initial tribute:

> This dedication was written while the dear friend and great Poet to whom it was addressed yet lived. It is left as he saw it-the last verses of mine that were ever to pass under his eyes. F.T.[10]

DEDICATION
To Coventry Patmore

Lo, my book thinks to look Time's leaguer down,
Under the banner of your spread renown!
Or if these levies of impuissant rhyme
Fall to the overthrow of assaulting Time,
Yet this one page shall fend oblivious shame,
Armed with your crested and prevailing Name.

Thompson's opening poem in the collection, *The Mistress of Vision*, is an exquisite fantasy that weaves into its narrative more than a hint of psychic significance. It begins with a description of paradise where within dwells *The Mistress of Vision*. Such a highly personal and keenly felt statement sees the poet very much allegorizing his own life and struggles. Like many of the other poems featured, *The Mistress of Vision* shows its creator developing a greater discipline than he subsequently allows himself in *Any Saint and The Dread of Height*. This new outlook brings a tightly-knit cohesion to the middle sequence of eight poems, entitled *A Narrow Vessel*, all prompted by the poet's recent abortive relationship with Maggie Brien, wherein, for the first time, he reveals his own sexual inadequacy.

Notable among the miscellaneous odes is *Anthem of Earth*, a somewhat arresting experiment in blank verse, which though occasionally bordering on Jacobean pastiche, gives yet further evidence of the poet's increasing command and control over both language and thought. No less so his much revised, *Ode to the Setting Sun*, written long before Thompson had met or been influenced by the work of Coventry Patmore, and providing the first fruit of his withdrawal from opium. Within the *Prelude*, the setting sun is vividly seen as a bubble of fire that drops slowly. In the *Ode* proper, the note of sadness is continued; the mystical twins of Time, Death and Birth, now gradually intruding further into the poet's consciousness.

The third poem within the opening sequence, *By The Reason of Thy Law*, takes its title from *De Profundis*, the sixth of the seventh penitential psalms, often used as a prayer for the dead. Likewise, *Orient Ode* has its origins very firmly within the Easter liturgy, which twelve months earlier had inspired the creation of one of his finest, yet little known works, *From The Night of Forebeing*. A remarkable eighteen pages in length, it is prefaced by two quotations. The first, from Sir Thomas Browne provides the title, and is closely followed by a line from the opening chapter of St John's Gospel: Et lux in tenebris erat, et tenebrae eam non comprehenderunt. (And the light shone in the darkness and in the darkness did not comprehend of it.)

Amid all the sometimes rather overwhelming religious symbolism inherent within the vast majority of the poetry, there remain a number of more unusual yet endlessly fascinating works. One such is *Memorat Memoria*, powerful lines addressed to the street girl who had befriended him some ten years earlier. Here he demonstrates no lessening of the intensity of his feelings towards her, after all, he always believed that he owed the first promise of his poetic career to her love. The *Ultima* sequence of eight poems, forms the closing section of the volume. It offers a counter balance to the opening, *Love in Dian's Lap*, appearing in his very first published volume some four years earlier. The subject is again Alice Meynell. Here he laments her indifference while still praising her many qualities.

Envoy closes this, the poet's third collection. Its last two lines give the key to much of the poetry to which they are the *envoy*. For while we grieve at the sight of temporal loss, we find joy in the faith that looks beyond to eternal gain. It forms a constant and recurring theme, found most notably in *The Night of the Forebeing* and the *Ode to the Setting Sun*:

Go, songs, for ended is our brief, sweet play;
Go, children of swift joy and tardy sorrow:
And some are sung, and that was yesterday.
And some unsung, and that may be to-morrow.
Go Forth; and if it be o'er stony way,
Old joy can lend what newer grief must borrow:
And it was sweet, and that was yesterday,
And sweet is sweet, though purchased with sorrow.
Go, songs, and come not back from your far way:
And if men ask you why ye smile and sorrow,
Tell them ye grieve, for your hearts know To-day,
Tell them ye smile, for your eyes know To-morrow.

While the actual sales figures for *New Poems* once again disappointed, the critics, most notably Arthur Quiller-Couch, were even more hostile than before. As usual, almost without exception, they concentrated on the linguistic excesses of the more challenging poetry rather than taking a broad overview of the work as a whole. However, none denied Thompson his place among the leading poets of the era. While there was even brief talk of a possible fourth volume, even Thompson came to realise that *New Poems* had effectively terminated his work as the poet that he had been called upon to be. In one of his many letters, he would write to Wilfrid Meynell, *"I am greatly lost in fire and glow. 'Tis time that I was silent. This book carries me quite as far as my dwindling strength will allow; and if I wrote further in poetry, I should write down my own fame."*[11]

Despite such protestations, occasional new work did indeed follow, beginning with the Manchester Guardian's request for a poem to celebrate Queen Victoria's Diamond Jubilee. Here, amid the occasional flash of Thompsonian rhetoric of yesteryear, the poet took the opportunity to pay tribute to some of his fellow practitioners: Tennyson, Browning, the Rossetti's, Christina and her brother Gabriel, Matthew Arnold and, of course, Coventry Patmore;

Last came a shadow tall, with drooping lid,
Which not yet hid
The steel-like flashing of his armèd glance;
Alone he did advance,
And all the throngs gave room
For one that looked with such a captain's mien.

A similar poem, *The Nineteenth Century*, was compiled for Lewis Hind, Editor of *The Academy*. Another, *Peace*, which celebrates the signing of a treaty in 1902 to mark the end of the South African War, had been commissioned some years earlier by the editor of the *Daily Chronicle*, so that it could printed once news of the treaty came through. One rather unexpected commission, again from Lewis Hind, was an ode to mark the sudden death of Cecil Rhodes on Monday, 26th March 1902[12]. This versified equivalent of an obituary editorial, most unusually for Thompson, was completed on time and within a mere three days. His editor later related its genesis:

> His chief regret was that his Muse had deserted him; so when on the morning after the death of Cecil Rhodes, I managed to lure him into the office and persuaded him that his Muse had not deserted him, and that he could write an Ode on the Death of Cecil Rhodes better than anybody else, he flushed and his strange eyes sparkled. However, I never learnt to count upon anything by Francis Thompson until it was actually in my hands. It was brought to me by a bewildered Thompson when the paper should have been going to press, in various pieces written on the backs of envelopes and toilet paper, produced from various pockets. I gave him half a crown to buy food, as in those days The Academy was his banker. I pieced the pieces of the Ode together and had them put into type. When Francis Thompson returned an hour or so later, flushed and momentarily easy in body, he read the proof swaying (I can see him now) and said in his slow, distinct enunciation, a little blurred maybe, at that moment, "It's all right, Hind, No corrections."[13]

In contrast, a further work, *To the English Martyrs*, would take him five months to complete. It stands out from his newspaper odes both in subject matter as well as treatment. First published in *The Dublin Review* of April 1906, it remains one of the few poems of any consequence that Thompson wrote after the appearance of *New Poems* in 1897. Some three hundred Catholics are known to have died during the English Reformation, many of whom met their end on the infamous Tyburn Gallows on the Edgware Road. When in London, Thompson himself would regularly pass the site on his way from his lodgings to the Meynell household. Genuinely moved by the courage of the many who died for their faith-Thomas More, Fisher, and countless others, here Thompson's thoughts are again intertwined with the long shadow cast by Calvary at Storrington.

While a large amount of Thompson's poetry in general and his cricket poetry in particular, remains little known, a similar fate would befall his rather curious version of the ancient poem, *Tom O'Bedlam*, found among his notebooks when he was briefly preparing a projected fourth volume of poetry. Thompson would totally rewrite the eight verses of this ancient work. First published in *The Dial*, Thompson's version appears nowhere in his collected works. Here for once, Thompson misjudges the mood as, in his hands, the poem's subject becomes something of a Romantic revivalist character, exchanging a moon struck innocence for a more down-at heel existence. The original needed no rewriting, least of all by Francis Thompson.

As Thompson himself once remarked in one of his numerous notebooks, "poets are men of inner weather, with their phases, seasons, tides, storms, calms, aridities and periods of fruitfulness". For his friend and early biographer, Everard Meynell, he was "A laureate among laureates", going on, with some justification to say that one can read Thompson's prefaces to his three volumes of poetry as if they were prefaces to thirty three, for so much of his poetry is about poetry itself. While a great deal of Thompson's output bears an indelible mark of his own era; much of it undoubtedly looks back to the metaphysical poets of the seventeenth century. But both in his poetry and prose, one also has glimpses of techniques and ideas which are contemporaneous with our own era.

Overall, his creative oeuvre divides neatly into four major categories: there are poems that deal with poetry, some with nature, others with people, while much the vast majority, in some way or other, relate to religion and religious ideas. Of these, some deal very specifically with man's relationship with God, while others approach and develop the topic in other ways. Having, after numerous false starts, fallen among friends, most notably the Meynell family, it was they who nurtured his talent, shared his faith and helped him find joy and delight throughout his continued exploration of mystical experiences. Latterly others, most notably Coventry Patmore and Katharine Tynan provided a no less beneficial support network.

As a poet of nature, Thompson, while capable of the occasionally vivid descriptive line, generally has little to say about the surface description of things. However, the background landscape of his output can often be a strange and violent one. One of his best poems of nature is *Contemplation* which, most unusually, demonstrates a poet able to assimilate detailed scientific knowledge into his poetry. As such, amid an outer stillness, an inner energy gradually permeates the texture. Here, within what might be termed *A Prayer of Quiet*, Thompson is at his most effective when illustrating seemingly ineffective detail within simple but direct language. Unlike many nineteenth century poets, Thompson is never unduly sentimental, even in small things.

Among the poems dealing with specific people are *Love in Dian's Lap* and *Ultima*, which focus on Alice Meynell, the *Ad Amicam* sonnets which relate to Katie King, while Maggie Brien is at the heart of *A Narrow Vessel.*

Collectively they make up the poet's spiritual autobiography. Each one of the adult poems celebrate relationships in which the feelings, while checked in real life, were able to run amok within the confines of poetry. Alice Meynell had long been his confidante and the inspirer of much of his poetry, but at all stages throughout their relationship, was inaccessible. While worthy of occasional mentions, she remains shadowy, the poet more generally concerned with reining in his own emotions.

For many, one of Thompson's finest works, once popular but now forgotten, yet surely now worthy of rediscovery, remains *An Arab Love Song*. The work, an oblique marriage proposal to Katie King, was written the day after Thompson had spent time with Wilfrid Blunt discussing Eastern love poetry. It first appeared in *The Dome* of January 1899. Here, for once, the poet achieves the maximum effect by the most economical of means. The opening of this simple love song so effectively conjures up the atmosphere of night, of mystery, and both beauty and expectancy. The image of the hunched camels links up with the last line of the poem, the girl taken to the heart of her lover where she will be secure.

The hunchèd camels of the night
Trouble the bright
And silver waters of the moon.
The Maiden of the Morn will soon
Through Heaven stray and sing,
Star gathering
Now, while the dark about our loves is strewn,
Light of my dark, blood of my heart, O come!
And night will catch her breath up, and be dumb.

Leave thy father, leave thy mother
And thy brother;
Leave the black tents of thy tribe apart!
Am I not thy father and thy brother,
And thy mother?
And thou – what needest with thy tribe's black tents
Who hast the red pavilions of my heart?

While quite satisfying as a simple love song, as always with Thompson, a deeper meaning lies beyond the more obvious. The first six lines of the final section are reminiscent of the Gospels (Matthew XII, 50 and Mark X, 28-30) in which Christ calls his followers to leave brethren and parents for His sake. The night under whose cover the lovers are to meet is also the night of this life in which the soul must give itself to Christ before the dawning of Eternity. Here the dawn is not here spoken of with any hostility as in other night love poems. Beneath the outward simplicity, one can trace a considerable density of meaning. The images work particularly well together as they do on all levels of significance.

As his early biographer, Everard Meynell so perceptively stated, "a great deal of Thompson's poetry is concerned with his own experience as a poet".[14] While his range may have been limited, however, within it he moved with great assurance and certainly of effect. Through the medium of such works as *Sister Songs*, *Contemplation*, *From the Night of Forebeing* and *The Cloud's Swan Song*, he proves more than capable of telling his readers what it feels like to be a poet. With regard to poetic inspiration, Thompson once revealingly wrote, "The insight of the poet springs from intuition, which is the highest reason, and is acquired through contemplation, which is the highest effort."[15] Throughout he deliberately links poet and mystic. He went on, "The weapon of the poet or saint is intuition, and contemplation is the state, the attitude which disposes the mind to receive intuition."[16]

Elsewhere in yet another of his numerous notebooks Thompson writes; "A mystic poet who is a vaporous fancy will not go far. Every such poet should be able to give a clear and logical prose resumé of his teaching as terse as a page of scholastic philosophy".[17] Of his own talents, he firmly believed himself to have been given unusual insights into spiritual facts, but at the same time, was often all too aware of the inadequacy of the response he made to fulfil that vision. In the Preface to *New Poems*, which he subsequently cancelled, he modestly disclaimed any higher intention: "the first section, exhibits mysticism in limited and varying degrees. I feel my instrument yet too imperfect to profane by it the higher ranges."

Amid an increasing pall of opium, little poetry of substance followed the appearance of *New Poems*. For this last decade of his all too short life Thompson now turned, with increasing success, to prose. His mentor, Wilfrid Meynell, had persuaded Lewis Hind, editor of *The Academy* to employ him as a reviewer and critic. Now back in London and keen to free himself financially from the Meynell purse strings, as well as *The Academy*, Thompson also wrote extensively for *The Athenaeum*, *The Daily Chronicle*, *The Dublin Review*, *Merry England*, *The New Review*, *The Outlook*, *The Weekly Register* and *The Tablet*. As well as literary subjects his wandering brief took in science, history, biography, politics and, of course, occasionally, cricket.

Here the great names of English literature would invariably be treated as personal friends. Having studied what became his immense prose output, totalling almost five hundred articles, the critic, Pierre Danchin commented, "Anyone who reads these reviews, written week after week for a period of ten years must be continually surprised and must feel a profound admiration for the writer's immense knowledge: he is not only familiar with all the important facts of English literary history but knows the works themselves."[18] Thompson, knowledgeable too about French literature, also handled Italian, Greek Roman and even Indian literature with his customary aplomb. Never fazed by more contemporary works, each is judged on its merits.

He gave a particularly warm welcome to both William Butler Yeats and G.K. Chesterton. However, his judgement was not infallible as, like many, he was generally dismissive of the work of Emily Dickinson. Writing on Crashaw, so influential within his own output, he writes, "So rare an artist, he was also an unsteady artist, of the most capricious taste."[19] Of Coleridge, Thompson responds most unsympathetically, while reviewing Davidson's *The Testament of an Empire Builder* he found, "too much metrical dialectic."[20] Similarly, he wrote that Laurence Housman had a "too deliberate manner" as well as a lack of "subtle intellectuality."[21] Unsurprisingly, he greatly admired the critical method of Thomas de Quincey.

Thompson's treatment of John Bunyan, "inexhaustible invention but no imagination,"[22] has often been cited as an example of how the poet's Catholic concerns were allowed to interfere with his critical objectivity. However, it perhaps should not be forgotten that the article he wrote on Bunyan was intended for a Catholic journal and therefore might be expected to draw on theological argument. Far from allowing his religious outlook to affect his judgement, Thompson often gives the reader the impression of making a deliberate effort to avoid any such inference. Studiously eschewing theological tags within his reviews, he retained not only a sense of perspective but unfailing respect for aesthetic values.

The best-known of Thompson's prose writings remains his essay on Shelley, dating from his time at Storrington and initially rejected by *The Dublin Review*. Discovered in the author's papers after his death, it was eventually published posthumously in *The Dublin Review* of July, 1908. For the first time in its history, *The Dublin Review* went into a second edition. Twelve months later it was published as a separate booklet with a preface by George Wyndham, who enthusiastically described it as, "the most important contribution to pure Letters written in English during the last twenty years."[23] Regularly reprinted, while speaking in general terms, many would affirm the study to be Francis Thompson's best work, superior even to his extensive poetic output.

Shelley*

The Church, which was once the mother of poets no less than of saints, during the last two centuries has relinquished to aliens the chief glories of poetry, if the chief glories of holiness she has preserved for her own. The palm and the laurel, Dominic and Dante, sanctity and song, grew together in her soil: she has retained the palm, but forgone the laurel. And for this if song is itself responsible, we Catholics are not irresponsible. Poetry in its widest sense, and when not professedly irreligious, has been too much and too long among many Catholics either misprized or distrusted; too much and too generally the feeling has been that it is at best superfluous, at worst pernicious, most often dangerous. Once poetry was, as she should be, the lesser sister and helpmate of the Church; the minister to the mind, as the Church to the soul. But poetry sinned, poetry fell; and in place of lovingly reclaiming her, Catholicism cast her from the door to follow the feet of her pagan seducer. The separation has been ill for poetry; it has not been well for religion....

.....We ask, therefore, for a larger interest, not in purely Catholic poetry, but in poetry generally, poetry in its widest sense. We ask for it from the average instructed, morally hale Catholic, who is not liable to spiritual cold with every breath of outside air. We ask for it specially in the case of verse, of poetry proper, as a mere necessity, if Catholicism is ever to make any impression on this branch of English art. With few exceptions, whatsoever in our best poets is great and good to the non-Catholic, is great and good also to the Catholic; and though Faber threw his edition of Shelley into the fire and never regretted the act; though, moreover, Shelley is so little read among us that we can still tolerate in our churches the religious parody which Faber should have thrown after his three-volumed Shelley; - in spite of this, we are disposed to number among such exceptions that straying spirit of light.....

**The editor thinks that his reader will welcome this very remarkable posthumous essay in the precise form in which it was found among the papers of its author, the late Mr Francis Thompson. It lacks, of course, the author's final revision, and may contain a sentence here or there which Mr Thompson himself would not finally have endorsed without those omissions or qualifying phrases which a writer makes or adds before passing his work for publication. Such modifications cannot, however, be satisfactorily made by another hand, and only obvious corrections necessary for literary reasons have been made by the author's literary executor, Mr Wilfrid Meynell, to whose kindness The Dublin Review is indebted for the offer of the article – Editor.*

In the century or more since his death, Thompson's literary reputation changed perhaps more than that of his many contemporaries. Invariably writing in a way that was unmistakably and distinctively his very own, seldom perhaps would he ever again be compared to William Shakespeare. Despite being continually overwhelmed by his own travails, nevertheless he proved more than capable of producing work which, while rarely, if ever, at variance with Catholic orthodoxy, remains intensely personal and hugely challenging. Never can it be said that his output makes easy reading, be it in thought or in form, but when at his very best, both his poetry and his prose retain the power not only to proclaim the glory of God but, on occasion, to lift the human spirit into his very presence.

Chapter 6

CRICKETANA

> To the readers of the memoir of the late Francis Thompson which was printed just after his death in The Athenaeum for November 23, 1907, and which stands as preface to the volume of his Selected Poems just published, it must have come as a surprise to learn that this rapt celebrant of the soul was, if not himself a cricketer, a very keen student of the game. They would have felt surprise not because there is anything irreconcilable between the life spiritual and this noble past time, but because one naturally falls into the habit of thinking of men in one direction only and Thompson's name carried with it the idea rather of midnight visions than of the sunlight pitch.[1]

It was Madeline Meynell's brother-in-law, the celebrated and widely admired playwright, author, poet and cricket commentator, Edward Lucas, who first drew our attention to Francis Thompson's cricket poetry in an article published in *The Cornhill Magazine* of July 1908. Sadly, for far too long, this aspect of Thompson's creative output has remained rather ignored and seriously under-valued.

A member of a Quaker family, born in Brighton in 1868, Edward Verrall Lucas established himself as a newspaper journalist before spending thirty four years at *Punch Magazine*. While there, he famously introduced his colleague, A.A. Milne to the illustrator E.H. Shepard, with whom Milne subsequently collaborated on the famous *Winnie-the-Pooh* books. In 1897, Lucas married a fellow writer, the daughter of a U.S. Army Colonel, Florence Elizabeth Griffin. Together they compiled a delightful series of children's books. Lucas himself, both under his own name and that of F.W. Mark, wrote a large number of stage plays. These included the comedy, *The Same*

A.N. Hornby

R. G. Barlow

Lancashire, County Champions, 1881
A.N. Hornby seated third left. R.G. Barlow front row second left.

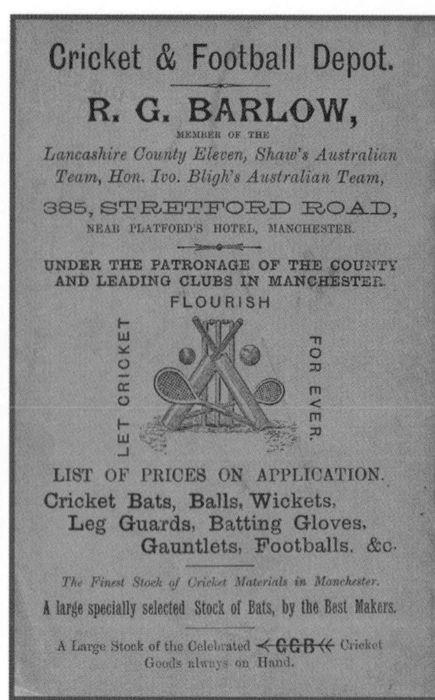

Above left: Stained glass window R.G. Barlow, Dick Pilling and A.N. Hornby
Above right: R.G. Barlow advertisement
Left: R G. Barlow pediment
Bottom: R.G. Barlow houses, Alderlea and, behind it, Glen May, Raikes Parade, Blackpool

A.N. Hornby

R.G. Barlow

W.G. Grace

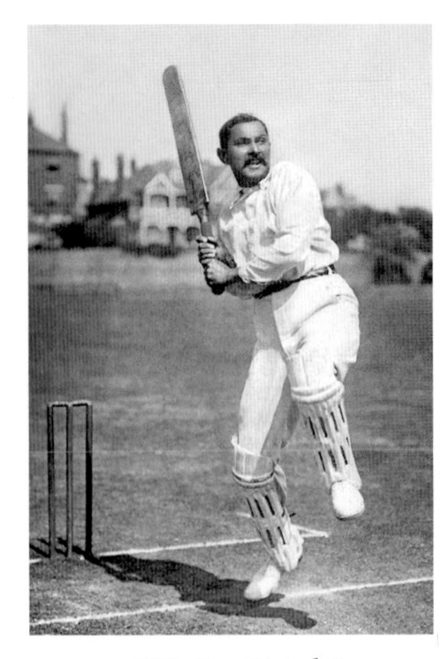

K.S. Ranjitsinhji

Fuller Pilch

Old Trafford Pavilion, 1868

A.H. Hornby

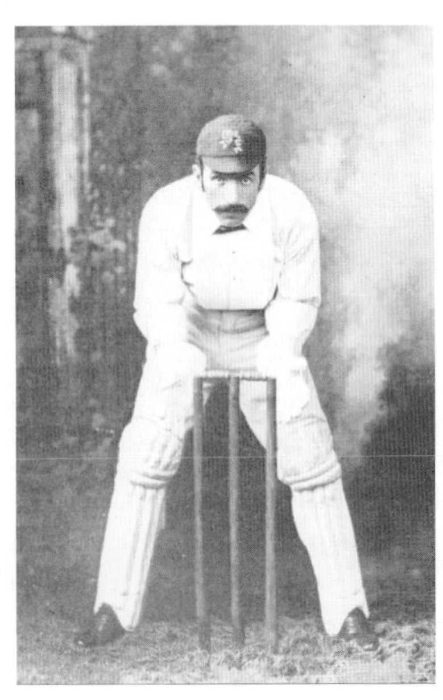

Dick Pilling

Star, which enjoyed somewhat limited success, as did, *The Visit of the King*, produced at the Palace Theatre in 1912.

Although cricket remained one of his great interests, Lucas thought and wrote of many other things. *The Open Road* (1899) was a collection of prose and verse about the English countryside. He also wrote about travel and art, the two subjects appearing together in his *Wanderer* books. Of these he produced volumes about London, Paris, Rome, Florence, Venice and Holland. Also among his output was a guide to British painters in the National Gallery and *A Wanderer Among the Pictures*, a volume devoted to the art galleries of Europe. A series, *Little Books on the Great Masters*, duly followed. Each of the eight volumes covering painters such as Michelangelo, Rembrandt and Leonardo da Vinci, among others. By now Lucas had taken charge of the publishing company of Methuen and Co.

As a noted writer and commentator on cricket matters himself, it is often overlooked that when Sir Herbert Baker, Sir Edwin Lutyens's colleague on the building of New Delhi, designed the new gates at Lord's as a memorial to W.G. Grace, he took his ideas of the sun and the cricket ball from Lucas's eloquent poem, *The Song of the Ball.* Throughout his initial article, Lucas seems genuinely delighted to find that Thompson too had shared the same passion. While long an admirer of the poet's religious output, he does everyone interested in the game a great service by revealing, for the very first time, hitherto unknown aspects of the poet's literary oeuvre. However, as was his wont, while constantly revelling in the game's rich heritage, Lucas proves to be something of a stranger to brevity:

> But literary genius and love of cricket have joined hands before, Cowper at Westminster was eager for the game. Byron played for Harrow against Eton. Mr Meredith, whose cricket enthusiasm flushes through his novels, was, he has told me, an alert fieldsman at the point of the bat; while Mr Barrie, it is well known, goes so far as to possess a team of his own whose merits he has described in an illustrated brochure which is at once the joy of those who own it and the despair of those who do not. Two instances of what I may call wholly unexpected cricketers may be added. Mr Lang, by whose cradle the muse of the game, benignantly smiling, most assuredly stood with gifts in her hand, has just discovered that Cuchulainn, the Irish hero, played, and naturally excelled, at cricket in its most primitive form about 200 A.D., while (and here we come nigher the poet of the Hound of Heaven) if you look in Mr Philip Norman's fascinating history of the West Kent Cricket Club you will find the name and fame of one H.E. Manning, afterwards Cardinal.

None the less it was a surprise to many persons, as I say, to find that Francis Thompson was a devotee too; and to those who had seen him in the flesh (and in the ulster which he did not don until the swallows were with us nor doff until they had flown) the surprise must have been greater still, since from such an exterior it would require a reader of men of supernatural acumen to deduce a love of open-air sport. For of all men Francis Thompson was to the casual observer least like a cricketer. It was not only this inverted affection for his overcoat; it was the whole effect, the ensemble as Whitman would say. If ever a figure seemed to say, "Take me anywhere in the world so long as it is not to a cricket match," that was Francis Thompson's. And his eye supported it. His eye had no brightness: it swung laboriously upon its object; whereas the enthusiasts of St John's Wood dart their glances like birds.

But Francis Thompson was born to baffle the glib inference. With his heart warmed by the very presence of God he could sell matches at Charing Cross. The world, which at every turn seemed to have crushed him beneath its cold weight, he had mastered and disdained while still a youth. Fate might beat against his frame but within blossomed the rose. He carried consolation about him. .... Cricket poetry hitherto has been descriptive, reflective, rapturous, gay, humorous. It has never before to my knowledge been made a vehicle for a lament for the past of profoundest melancholy.

Everyone knows the sadness of the backward look-everyone has lost friends both of kin and of the soul. But the cricket enthusiast (and this applies to other spectacular games and sports too), whether he plays or merely watches, has had two pasts, two chances of bereavement-his own private losses, and the losses that have been suffered by the game. It is impossible for a quite ordinary enthusiast to see one match without thinking of an earlier one: how much more then must a poet do so? The simplest and most prosaic of us, whose lives have been fortunate, cannot go to Lord's and regret no missing face upon the field. How have we, for example, yearned for Mr Stoddart these many seasons past! But Thompson..............[2]

This following untitled poem by Francis Thompson is a description in generally easy couplets of the famous encounter between Middlesex and Yorkshire which took place at Lord's between 29th and 31st May 1899. In his article, Lucas merely quotes two lengthy extracts, censoring what he feels to be Thompson's somewhat unwarranted questioning of the psychological state of the distinguished Yorkshire captain, Lord Hawke. As usual, with so much of Thompson's output, it remains questionable whether it was intended for publication, or more a versified memorandum of the game, created for the poet's own personal amusement. Nevertheless, it is an excellent example of his talents while, at the same time, recording a gladiatorial contest of epic proportions:

White sprinkle a-glitter 'gainst the sun,
With dark-clad silence gazing on,
Whence thunders break in unison,
Lo, what gusts shall in the shine be done!
Unbeaten South, unbeaten North,
On Lord's field come to the battle forth;
Unbeaten North goes down, ah me!
For a poor two hundred and some three,
Before the potent-to-overturn
Dread-bowling Trott, and Roche, and Hearne.
Five Middlesex wickets fallen, too,
For none too many, if none so few:
For the days are as batsmen love, pitch good
Whereon to make firm the stubborn wood.
Now, the second day, I who sing
Watch what the fortune of cricket shall bring-
Fortune of cricket, sterner far
Than is the partial fortune of war.
A Warner, who all month has slept,
By such shall ye at bay be kept,
Ye men of Yorkshire? For ye have too
O'erturners of wickets not a few.
Alas! This so-long-slumbrous-Warner
Has our best bowling in a corner;
Retires, with hundred, and fifty more,
'Midst clapping and loud-throated roar.
But he is gone, with roar and claps;
Now, say, are ended our evil haps,
Thou Hawke, who stand'st with fallen chaps?
Alack! to Trott M'Gregor comes forth,
Last state is worse than thy first, O North!
For Trott, who also month-long kept
Inert, as the batsman in him slept,
Wakes, and with tumult of his waking
The many-girded ground is shaking!
With rolling claps and clamour, as soar
Fours after fours, and ever four!
Bowls Rhodes, bowls Jackson, Haigh bowls, Hirst,-

To him the last is as the first:
West-end tent or pavilion-rail,
He lashes them home with a thresher's flail.
Says Hawke: "I would give the half I've got
To him who made yon devil's bird Trott!"
So spake, in the out-field where he stands,
My lord, with his clenchèd teeth and hands.
But, for fuming smother and vicious grin,
His men stay out, and those men stay in.
All the long noon, under the sun,
Those men hit out, and those men hit on,
And never are, but his side *is*-done.
Ha! Trott at last a chance has lent
In the long-field yonder,-sure heavenly-sent-
Sail down left of pavilion-tent.
By all the-angels, the slave has dropped it!
Be Nemesis thanked, his hand has copped it!
As he shakes on the grass his fingers bloody,
Thinks Hawke: "I would it were all in your body!
Your blind bat-blink, my beauty gay,
Will cost us seventy runs today!"
Trott keeps them trotting, till his d------d score
Is just one hundred, sixty, and four,-
The highest tally this match has scored
And the century fourth is long up on the board.
Thank heaven, the fellow's grown reckless now,
Jumps and slogs at them anyhow:
Two narrow shaves, amid frenzied howl
Of jubilant people, and lordly growl;
Till a clinker tingles in Brown's left hand-
Good Brown! You have snapped the infernal stand!
The last two wickets go tedious down,
And my lord strides off with his teeth and frown.

Yorkshire batted first totalling 203 as the Middlesex bowlers, Hearne and Trott shared five wickets apiece. Replying against a Yorkshire attack comprising Wilfred Rhodes, Schofield Haigh, George Hirst and Rt. Hon. Stanley Jackson, opener Pelham Warner paved the way by making a historic 150. Overshadowing him, however, was Albert Trott with a remarkable innings of 164. At one point he had scored 137 out of 181 in an hour and a half. In the process, he passed his previous highest score in the county championship, completed a first century in the competition, and improved on his previous top score in all first class matches. Thompson even mentions one of his many drives that hit the pavilion rails so hard that the ball ricocheted back to a stationary Jackson at mid-on.

Born in Melbourne in 1873, Albert Edwin Trott, was the most promising Australian cricketer of his generation. Disappointed at not being selected to tour England in 1896, when his elder brother, Harry served as Captain, he came to England on his own account, joined the Lord's ground staff and qualified for Middlesex. He was tall and strong, a hard-hitting middle order batsman and right arm fast medium bowler. When playing for MCC against the touring Australians in 1899, he famously hit a ball over the top of the Lord's pavilion. Having won three test caps for Australia, he later made a further two appearances for England. After retiring, he became a first class umpire. However, while struggling with increasing health problems in later life, on 30 July 1914, he shot himself. He was aged just 42.

The following poem entitled *Rime O' Bat of My Sky-Em*, is a parody of Edward Fitzgerald's *Rubáiyát of Omar Khayyam* and a rare example of Thompson's capacity for humorous verse. Here again it was first published in Edward Lucas's survey of Francis Thompson's cricket verse. Despite his known unreliability as an editor, Lucas was perhaps right when he added; "Thompson's mind was too powerful and proud for imitation or sustained *facetioe*, and he quickly became individual and human, so that the stanzas although a parody in form are also a new and independent thing. They seem to have no little charm".

Part 1

Wake! for the Ruddy Ball has taken flight
That scatters the slow Wicket of the Night;
　　And the swift Batsman of the Dawn has driven
Against the Star-spiked Rails a fiery Smite.
Wake, my Beloved! take the Bat that clears
The sluggish Liver, and Dyspeptics cheers:
　　To-morrow? Why, to-morrow I may be
Myself with Hambledon and all its Peers.

To-day a Score of Batsmen brings, you say?
Yes, but where leaves the Bats of Yesterday?
　　And this same summer day that brings a Knight
May take the Grace and Ranjitsinjh away.

Willsher the famed is gone with all his 'throws,'
And Alfred's Six-foot Reach where no man knows;
　　And Hornby-that great hitter-his own Son
Plays in his place, yet recks not the Red Rose.

And Silver Billy, Fuller Pilch and Small,
Alike the pigmy Briggs and Ulyett tall,
Have swung their Bats an hour or two before,
But none played out the last and silent Ball.

Well let them Perish! What have we to do
With Gilbert Grace the Great, or that Hindu?
Let Hirst and Spooner slog them as they list,
Or Warren bowl his 'snorter'; care not you!

With me along the Strip of Herbage strown,
That is not laid or watered, rolled or sown,
Where name of Lord's and Oval is forgot,
And peace to Nicholas on his bomb-girt Throne.

A level Wicket, as the Ground allow,
A driving Bat, a lively Ball, and thou
Before me bowling on the Cricket-pitch-
O Cricket-pitch were Paradise enow!

Part II

I listened where the Grass was shaven small,
And heard the Bat that groaned against the Ball:
Thou pitchest Here and There, and Left and Right,
Nor deem I where the Spot thou next may'st Fall.

Forward I play, and Back, and Left and Right,
And overthrown at once, or stay till Night:
But this I know, where nothing else I know,
The last is Thine, how so the Bat shall smite.

This thing is sure, where nothing else is sure,
The boldest Bat may but a Space endure;
And he who One or who a Hundred hits
Falleth attending to thy Force or Lure.

Wherefore am I allotted but a Day
To taste Delight, and make so brief a stay;
For need of all my Labour laid aside,
Ended alike the Player and the Play.

Behold, there is an Arm behind the Ball,
Nor the Bat's Stroke of its own Striking all;

And who the Gamesters, to what end the Game,
I think thereof our Willing is but small.

Against the Attack and Twist of Circumstance
Though I oppose Defence and shifty Glance,
What Power gives Nerve to me, and what Assaults,-
This is the Riddle. Let dull Bats cry 'Chance.'

Is there a Foe that [domineers] the Ball?
And one that Shapes and wields us Willows all?
Be patient if Thy Creature in Thy Hand
Break, and the so-long-guarded Wickets fall!
Thus spoke the Bat. Perchance a foolish Speech
And wooden, for a Bat has straitened Reach:
Yet thought I, I had heard Philosophers
Prate much on this wise, and aspire to Teach.

Ah, let us take our Stand, and Play the Game,
But rather for the Cause than for the Fame;
Albeit right evil is the Ground, and we
Know our Defence thereon will be but lame.

O Love, if thou and I could but Conspire
Against this pitch of Life, so false with Mire,
Would we not Doctor it afresh, and then
Roll it out smoother to the Bat's Desire?

The poem itself contains mention of numerous people and places involved in nineteenth century cricket. Hambledon is the historic Hampshire village where cricket first became a recognised sport. Between 1750 and 1791 it dominated and developed the game until its power base moved to London. Something of a poet who wrote prose, Albert E. Knight was also a professional cricketer with Leicestershire. A religious man and a Sunday school teacher, when he came to the wicket to bat, he would take guard then lean for a moment or two over his bat with his eyes closed. Waiting to bowl, Walter Brearley asked his captain what the problem was? "He's just saying his little prayer," replied MacLaren. "And what's he praying for?" asked Brearley. "Well," whispered MacLaren, "I suppose he's praying for a century." Whereupon Brearley exploded, "I'll write to the bloody MCC over this!"

Willsher was Edgar Willsher, The Lion of Kent, and a member of the All England team in 1828. To the name of Alfred, Francis Thompson has added a footnote: 'Alfred is Alfred the Great, Alfred Mynn, W.G. of his day; six feet two, mutton of shoulder fist, foot on which he leaned made a grave in soft turf, brilliant both as a bat and fast bowler'. Born at Goudhurst in Kent in 1807, Mynn died at Thurnham in 1861. There were two Smalls, both Hambledon men while Silver Billy was the illustrious, William Beldham, also a prominent member of the Hambledon Club. Fuller Pilch, a Norfolk man by birth, was the best batsman in England between 1820 and 1850. He died at Canterbury in 1870. His epitaph reads 'Land of Hops, you hold in trust. Very sacred human dust!'

The Hornby mentioned in the poem is Albert Henry Hornby, A.N.'s son, who, in that particular year, 1908, had just acceded to the Lancashire Captaincy. Born on 29th July 1877, and educated at Harrow and Trinity College, Cambridge, he first played for the county in 1899, a year that marked the end of his father's career but ensured that a Hornby stayed in the Lancashire team for almost half a century. Father and son played together only once, against Leicestershire when A.H. opened the innings and scored 18, only to be outshone by his father, then aged 52, who went in at number nine and hit 53 in an hour. A right hand attacking batsman rather in the manner of his father, and although an occasional opening bat, he usually appeared down the order. Like his father, he too played the game for fun.

Initially somewhat overwhelmed by his heritage, Hornby succeeded Archie MacLaren as Lancashire Captain in 1908, remaining in post until the outbreak of the Great War. In the end, although he did not follow Hornby senior into the England team, he played 283 times for Lancashire, only nine fewer than father, scored eight centuries to his father's ten, but when he finished in 1914, he actually had a better average by two tenths of a run! A fine horseman, he subsequently lived for a time at Nettleville, Killinardrushin County Cork where he served as the Master of the Muskberry Hunt. Marrying Esme Lonsdale in 1915, their two sons, Michael and Albert, were both tragically killed in action during the course of the Second World War. Retiring to live at Kilworth in Leicestershire, Albert Henry Hornby died there, aged 75, in 1952.

Another outstanding sportsman of the era, who also played football for Sheffield Wednesday, was Yorkshire all-rounder, George Ulyett. Famously dubbed, 'Happy Jack', it was said Yorkshire played him for his whistling and England played him to go in first with W.G. Grace, to give the doctor confidence. Briggs was, of course Johnny Briggs, one of the best loved of Lancashire cricketers, whose enthusiasm proved infectious for spectators and team alike. Tragically suffering from a form of epilepsy, he had a seizure during the Leeds Test Match of 1899. When later confined to Cheadle Asylum, there it was said that he would imagine himself bowling up and down the ward.

At the end of every day before going to bed, he would proudly announce his bowling figures to the nurses. He died, aged 39, in 1902.

This next offering, *The Little Red Rose Shall Pale at Last*, was first published in Everard Meynell's *Life of Francis Thompson*. According to Meynell, the reference in the last line is to the London area of Marylebone. As Thompson walked home each night from the Meynell's house to his lodgings, he would pass through this area, often composing poetry as he went. Six men bearing the name Tyldesley represented Lancashire in the county championship, four brothers from Westhoughton and two from Worsley. These last two, John Thomas and George Ernest were, for forty years, the heart and soul of the Lancashire batting. Alongside them was one of the outstanding fast bowlers of his era, Walter Brearley. Nowadays his outstanding ability has been somewhat overshadowed by his seemingly interminable run-ins with the cricketing authorities.

The little Red Rose shall be pale at last.
What made it red but the June wind's sigh?
And Brearley's ball that he bowls so fast?
It shall sink in the dust of the late July!

The pride of the North shall droop at last;
What made her proud but the Tyl-des-lie?
An Austral ball shall be bowled full fast,
And baffle his bat and pass it by.

The Rose once wounded shall snap at last.
The Rose long bleeding it shall not die.
This song is secret. Mine ear it passed
In a wind from the field of Le-Bone-Marie.

Another little-known work, *Sons, Who Have Sucked Stern Nature Forth*, was similarly featured first in Everard Meynell's, *Life of Francis Thompson*. Among the cricketers mentioned here is Frank Sugg, a tall and dashing batsman, who played county cricket for Lancashire, Yorkshire and Derbyshire. He was also a footballer with Sheffield Wednesday, among others. Fellow Lancashire team mates included four Steel brothers and three Eccles, all amateurs and unrelated, Alexander, Henry and Joseph. Of the Wards, there were two, again unrelated, Albert and Frank. Albert, a schoolteacher, Leeds born but qualifying by residence, was a more than useful leg break bowler. He also formed a most productive opening partnership with Frank Sugg. While Sugg's combative style soon saw him likened to Albert Neilsen Hornby, the more cerebral Ward, became a latter day Richard Gorton Barlow.

> Sons, who have sucked stern nature forth
> From the milk of our firm-breasted north!
> Stubborn and stark in whatever field,
> Stand, sons of the Red Rose, who may not yield!
>
> Gone is Pattison's lovely style,
> Not the name of him lingers awhile.
> O Lancashire Red Rose, O Lancashire Red Rose!
> The men who fostered thee, no man knows.
> Many bow to thy present shows,
> But greater far have I seen thee, my Rose!
>
> Thy batting Steels, D.G., H.B.,
> Dost thou forget? And him, A.G.,
> Bat superb, of slows the prince,
> Father of all slow bowlers since?
>
> Yet, though Sugg, Eccles, Ward, Tyldesley play
> Thy part of a great, a vanished day,
> By this may ye know, and long may ye know,
> Our Rose; it is greatest when hope is low.
> The Lancashire Red Rose, O The Lancashire Red Rose!
> We love the hue on her cheek that shows:
> And it never shall blanch, come the world as foes,
> For dipt in our hearts is the Lancashire Red Rose!

Here in this next offering, Thompson's title can literally be translated as, *Day of Judgement, The Day is Near*. Unusually for the poet, the verses offer a Lancastrian's rare paean of praise to the White Rose county. Here once again, the source is his fellow writer, Everard Meynell. They bear the subtitle *(July 16, '98; Mote Park and Old Trafford)* and not as Brigid Boardman's 2001 edition states, More Park.[3] While Lancashire were then the current county champions, 1898 proved to be particularly memorable for Yorkshire as they went on to take the county championship title in convincing style. However, on the 16th July, they suffered a rare loss, losing to Kent by six wickets at Mote Park, Maidstone. It was also the year that the county first discovered a rosy-cheeked aspiring young bowler from Kirkheaton, the soon to be legendary, Wilfred Rhodes.

Dies Irae, Dies Illa
(July 16,'98; Mote Park and Old Trafford)

Woe is me, fair White Rose!
It is a bitter stead,
That thou should'st fall unto false Southron,
And not to thy Sister Red!

Woe is me, my Red, Red Rose!
Woe and shameful plight,
When the Red Rose falls to the South blast
And not to the Rose of White!

When Red Rose met White on Bramhall grass
And turned not back from each other; alas,
Had the Red Rose smote the White Rose,
Or the White Rose smote the Red,
Or ever bent to the soft Southron,
The stubborn Northern Head!

O Red Rose, O White Rose,
Set you but side by side,
And bring against you the leaguèd South,
You might their shock abide;
Yea, bring against you the banded South,
With all their strength allied.
My White Rose, my Red Rose
Could smite their puissance i' the mouth!

Between 1855 and 1973, Bramhall Lane, home of Sheffield United Football Club, also echoed to the merry sound of Yorkshire cricket throughout the summer months. It was there in July 1898, that the Roses encounter was given as a benefit game for the admirable all-rounder, Ted Wainwright. The Yorkshire first innings was built around a brilliant 144 from J.T. Brown, while Lancashire's involved some brilliant hitting from Sugg and Cuttell. Declaring at 253 for 3, Yorkshire asked their opponents to make nearly 300 in three hours. Only a bold effort, particularly by Willis Cuttell, who scored 125 in the match without ever losing his wicket in either innings, saved them from defeat. While not having the better of the two Roses encounters that year, they would be A.N. Hornby's last as Lancashire Captain.

Stand fast, stand fast, my bonny red rose,
Your evil fate contemn!
For one cold blast can your leaves be strown,
And the red rose fall from its stem?

This isolated stanza appears to have been the poet's rallying call to his beloved county in the wake of a rare defeat. It was found by Father Terence Connolly in one of Thompson's many notebooks housed in the Boston College Collection. It was first published in 1944, in the author's account of his visit to England some six years earlier, which he entitled, *Francis Thompson: In His Paths.*[4] Somewhat ironically, while Connolly was staying with the Meynell family came news of the death in a London nursing home of E.V. Lucas on 26th June 1938. Having lived alone for many years, all through his final illness he refused to allow any of his friends to visit him. In addition, he requested no religious ceremony at his funeral. For the Meynell family, Lucas's death revived many past painful memories.

It is often overlooked that Francis Thompson also wrote occasional prose on the game, most notably a lengthy critique of *The Jubilee Book of Cricket* by K.S. Ranjitsinhji, that first appeared in *The Academy* on 4th September 1897. A most conscientious reviewer, as here, every facet of his subject would be considered before he formed an opinion. Long neglected, the feature, entitled *A Prince of India on The Prince of Games*, is notable for the author's technical acumen. Alongside a minute examination of the difference between the pitched-up balls of the underarm bowler and other matters, the author also pays fulsome tribute to the former Lancashire cricketer, Rev Vernon Royle. Having subsequently taken Holy Orders, during his later career as a school master, Royle was responsible for the early education of Albert Neilsen Hornby's youngest son, the future world traveller and explorer, John.[5]

REVIEWS

A PRINCE OF INDIA ON THE PRINCE OF GAMES

The Jubilee Book of Cricket. By K. S. Ranjitsinhji. (Blackwood & Sons)

There is more than a mere publisher's appropriateness in the title of this book. This Jubilee year is the apogee of the British Empire; it may also fairly be considered as the apogee of cricket. The art of preparing consummate wickets-wickets which make batting an ease and a delight, bowling a game of patience and endurance-has reached its height. A brilliantly sunny summer has done such wickets full justice; and a wonderful fertility of consummate batsmen has taken full advantage of the wickets and the weather. Yet-extraordinary to relate-it has also been a year in which bowlers have distinguished themselves. A race of bowlers has arisen capable of coping with these conditions. It might be supposed that they would be solely slow or at least medium-pace bowlers. But not so. Three of the most successful bowlers of the season have been Richardson, Mold and Kortright-all three fast bowlers. What it means, in the way of endurance, for a fast bowler to keep up pace and length through these enormous innings, on wickets enough to numb the pluck of any bowler, only a thorough cricketer can understand. Yet another consideration completes the appropriateness of the title. The peculiar feature of the Jubilee has been the way in which it has drawn attention to the bonds between England and its great dependencies: and the batsman of the day who is acknowledged to be the most consummate in style and all-round power(though he may not be at the head of the averages) is an Indian Prince. This batsman, Prince Ranjitsinhji (perhaps the finest who has appeared in England, except Grace), is the author of this *Jubilee Book of Cricket.* A native of India teaches Englishmen their own national game; and they all, with one accord, hasten to sit at his feet. He is not only a practical master in the game, but he has analysed it as a critic analyses the laws of literature. The book is illustrated with a profusion of instantaneous photographs of the principal cricketers, showing their attitude in bowling, fielding, wicket-keeping, or play as batsman, which would alone render it uniquely valuable. And the whole range of cricket is covered with the utmost minuteness by Prince Ranjitsinhji's pen. Training and outfit, fielding in all its branches, bowling, batting, captaincy, and umpiring are the principal divisions of his work.

No details are too minute for his consideration. For example, in the outset of the chapter on batting he instructs the batsman how to choose his bat, and with regard to his choice of batting-gloves and leg-guards.

And very valuable his advice will be found. He has subjected everything, in fielding, bowling, and batting, to an unprecedented process of analysis, which for the first time provides us with a text-book at all points corresponding to modern needs. The older books were in effect based on the laws handed down from the times of under hand bowling. But the methods of modern good-length bowling, with off and leg-break, a crowded off-field, and few chances for leg-hitting you will seek in vain for them. The "pull" is mentioned by them only to be reprobated. Prince Ranjitsinhji discards tradition and teaches the game as it is now played. The "pull" and the "hook" figure largely in his instructions, and he is justly severe on the coaches who ban both as illegitimate. Nevertheless, there was real reason, which he does not recognise, for the proscription of these strokes by the old players. He himself recognises that they are dangerous off a fast bowler, even on a true wicket, and that on a wicket rendered slippery by rain which has affected the surface, or a "sticky" wicket, they must be eschewed. Now the rough character of the old wickets always enabled the bowler to get plenty of work on the ball, and so the "pull" or the "hook" were really rash and ruinous strokes, were the wicket as dry as you please.

Detailed criticism of a work covering minutely the whole range of cricket is impossible in a review. I can offer only a few scattered commentaries on particular points. Prince Ranjitsinhji has done well to place fielding foremost, in the hope, as he says, that by so doing he may stimulate attention to the most neglected, yet very important, branch of the cricketer's art. Fine fielding is very largely the work of a captain who is himself a fine fielder, and knows its vast importance in winning matches. Many a match has been won rather in the field than at the wicket. And, if only a boy will set himself really to study its niceties, it is a most fascinating branch of cricket. Prince Ranjitsinhji remarks on the splendid opportunities of cover-point, and cites the Rev. Vernon Royle as the cover-point to whom all cricketers give the palm during the last thirty years. "From what one hears," he says, "he must have been a magnificent fielder." He was. And I notice the fact, because Vernon Royle may be regarded as a concrete example of the typical fielder, and the typical fielder's value. He was a pretty and stylish bat; but it was for his wonderful fielding tha the was played. A ball for which hardly another cover-point would think of trying, he flashed upon, and with a single action stopped it and returned it to the wicket. So placed that only a single stump was visible to him, he would throw that down with unfailing accuracy, and without the slightest pause for aim. One of the members of the Australian team in Royle's era, playing against Lancashire, shaped to start for a hit wide of cover-point. "No, no!" cried his partner; "the policeman is there!" There were no short runs anywhere in the neighbourhood of Royle. He simply terrorised the batsmen; nor was there any necessity for an extra cover-now so constantly employed. In addition to his sureness and swiftness, his style was a miracle of grace. Slender and symmetrical, he moved with the lightness of a young roe, the flexuous elegance of a leopard-it was a sight for an artist or a poet to see him field. Briggs, at his best, fell not far short in efficiency; but there was no comparison between the two in style and elegance. To be a fielder like Vernon Royle is as much worth any youth's endeavours as to be a batsman like Ranjitsinhji, or a bowler like Richardson.

In the chapter on bowling Prince Ranjitsinhji shows that he has studied this art as closely as his own art of batting. He is full of wise counsel with regard to all the styles of bowling, and their relation to the various kinds of wickets and batsmen. Nothing in his book is more useful than his analysis of a typical game on a good wicket (from a bowler's standpoint) between two first-class sides. The batting side, under thinly disguised names, is easily to be recognised as Surrey; the bowling side, from the absence of names, is harder to be recognised. It is evidently an actual match which the writer had the chance of observing; therefore, it is possible that the other side may be Sussex. I am glad to see that Prince Ranjitsinhji, showing in this the independence and actuality which he displays throughout his book, does not think it beneath him to recognise the possible value of lob-bowling, to expound its principles, and recommend its cultivation by cricketers who are that way inclined. He even goes so far as to surmise that other kinds of under-arm bowling might prove baffling to present-day batsmen if they were revived. I am of opinion that this would certainly be the case. On one point I think that the author does not quite bring out the peculiarities of under-arm. Namely, that "good length bowling" is not as continuously necessary to under-arm as to over-arm bowling. Now, I think that the under-arm bowler can afford to pitch his balls well up, more than the over-arm bowler can; and that it often pays to do so-at least, against the present race of batsmen, who are unaccustomed to under-arm. For two reasons. In the first place, the over-arm bowler shrinks from pitching his balls up on account of the extra exertion involved. He does so only occasionally, as Prince Ranjitsinhji states, on account of this exertion. The under-arm bowler, on the contrary, because of the ease and naturalness of his action, can pitch his balls well up without any difficulty. In the second place, because of the difference of trajectory between the two methods of bowling. An over-arm ball describes approximately a parabola, and when it is well pitched up comes therefore thoroughly onto the bat. But the drop of an under-arm ball, particularly if it be slow, is so much more sudden that it may comparatively and roughly be considered a straight drop. Even if fast or quick medium, it is much more abrupt in descent than a like over-arm ball. Consequently a batsman who attempts to clout a well-pitched-up under-arm as he would a like over-arm ball stands a fair chance of playing over it, especially when he is unaccustomed to this kind of bowling. If, on the other hand, he plays back, it is difficult to get the ball away. So that he may be deceived, and if he adopts caution is not likely to score off the ball. Yorkers, again, are perfectly easy to an under-arm bowler; they put no great strain on the weakest arm. Admirable are all the author's lessons on bowling, had we space to follow them; and admirable his concluding declaration that it is head-work, and the study of the batsman's peculiarities, which puts the crown on a bowler.

"There are bowlers," he says, "who for some reason or other seem to fascinate the batsman, and make him do what they want in spite of himself.......The batsman has to fight not only against the particular ball bowled, but against a mysterious unseen influence. There are 'demon' bowlers in more senses than one. They are few and far between; but when they come, they win matches by their own individual might."

In other words, genius tells in cricket as in all else.

In batting, Prince Ranjitsinhji is on his own ground, and his instructions are up to the latest date. He dwells on forward play in a manner not to be met in the older treatises, though he confesses that his own predilections (as might be expected from a player so quick of eye and supple of wrist) are towards back play. His minute and perfect instructions must be sought in the book. Only one point I will comment on, because it is not borne out in the illustrations, though the author seems to imagine it is. He says, quite truly, that the position of the left(that is, the upper) hand should be changed in the forward stroke. That is, the left hand should be shifted round the bat, so that the finger-tips are presented towards the bowler, instead of the back of the hand, as in the ordinary position of holding the bat. Some players, he allows do not so twist the upper hand round the bat in playing forward. He refers to the illustrations to exemplify the action. But, unless my eyes are deceived, all the batsmen here photographed in the act of playing forward have the left hand unchanged. If so, it is a singular chance; for there can be no doubt of its advantage. The position of the hand may be understood by reference to the portrait of Prince Ranjitsinhji playing back; for here he has the left hand shifted round as it should be in forward play. It is advisable, above all, in forward defensive play. And this because it guards against the two chief dangers in such play. These are, that the bat may not be kept straight, so as to cover the stump from top to bottom: and that the tip of the blade may be pushed forward in advance of the upper portion of the blade, so as to put the ball up and give a catch. If the left hand be not shifted round, it exercises by its position a natural drag upon the handle of the bat, so as to deflect the upper portion of the blade to the left, and leave the superior portion of the stump exposed. Moreover, besides this lateral deflection of the handle, and consequently of the upper part of the blade, it also exercises a backward drag upon them, so as to leave the tip of the blade dangerously advanced, with the likelihood of a catch. Careful practice may overcome both these tendencies; but in a moment of excitement and inattention they are liable to assert themselves with ruinous results. Whereas the twisting of the left hand round the handle mechanically keeps the bat straight, and the upper portion of the blade well advanced over the lower. A single experiment and comparison will convince any player of this. Another point which may be learned by studying the various photographs of Prince Ranjitsinhji batting given in this book is, that a batsman will do well to alter the relative position of his hands in varying kinds of play. Thus, the Prince's ordinary position at the wicket is with the two hands together at the top of the handle; but in back play his right hand is slid down towards the blade. In glance-play back and forward, his right hand is apparently about two inches above the blade, but well separated from the left hand. Some batsmen, who go in for steady play, ordinarily keep the right hand a little above the blade, and apart from the left. Such a batsman, if he lunges forward to drive a ball, where an inch or two of reach makes all the difference, will do well to slide the right hand up to the left at the top of the handle, in order to get the full length of the bat in reaching out at the ball. In fact, any adaptable batsman will find the use of not keeping his hands in one uniform stiff position for all kinds of strokes. Here is part of the value of the instantaneous photographs in this book. It may be doubtful whether Prince Ranjitsinhji himself was conscious of this feature in his play-at least, he never mentions it; and so the photographs supply hints sometimes not given by the author.

Upon back play, and the methods of making it available for offensive purposes, the author is excellent. The subtlest and newest refinements of stroke all round the wicket are expounded with beautiful clearness: the drive to cover-point or extra-cover, the peculiar stroke with a horizontal bat between a forward-cut and a drive, leg-glances and forcing-strokes on the on-side; and, above all, those once condemned strokes, made possible by the perfection of modern wickets, the pull and the hook. These are described with a perfect lucidity only to be expected from a batsman who is himself a master of them. There is one very significant omission. The draw, that most stylish stroke of the older batsman, is never once described. The conditions of modern bowling have, indeed, rendered it obsolete. The last time I saw it used was by A.P. Lucas in a match between England and Australia. On wrist play, he is very strong, as might be supposed from the beautiful wrist player in England. But for all those niceties I can only refer the reader to the book, promising him, if he be a cricketer, that he has a rich treat of scientific analysis. Prince Ranjitsinhji's exclusive part is completed by two excellent chapters on Captaincy and Umpiring.

Fully another half of the book, however, is taken up by summary reviews of English cricket, under the headings of Public School, University, and County Cricket. The excellent introductory article on public school cricket is by Mr W.J. Ford; and then follow succinct accounts of all the chief public schools in England. Oxford cricket is admirably dealt with by the old Oxonian, Mr T. Case; and for Cambridge, Mr W.J. Ford again takes up the pen. The history of the MCC is dealt with; and then follow articles on all the counties, in many cases signed by leading exponents of county cricket, such as Mr Hornby in the case of Lancashire. One of the most attractive of all is that on Hampshire, on account of a long quotation from a very interesting article contributed by Mr E.V. Lucas to the *Morning Post* last year, dealing with the old Hambledon Club. Talk of modern enthusiasm for cricket! It is nothing to that of the ancients of the game. Witness this of the Rev. John Mitford, describing a visit he paid to Beldham's cottage, when that veteran of Hambledon and Surrey was in his last years:

"In his kitchen, black with age, hangs the trophy of his victories, the delight of his youth, the exercise of his manhood, and the glory of his age-his BAT. Reader, believe me when I tell you, I trembled when I touched it; it seemed an act of profaneness, of violation. I pressed it to my lips and returned it to its sanctuary."

Let that fine bit of rhodomontade put you in tune for approaching the best analysis of cricket yet produced, written by a magnificent cricketer. Some faults of get-up and in the reproduction of the photographs there are; but I have not the heart to particularise them.

FRANCIS THOMPSON.

Chapter 7

THE FIELD IS FULL OF SHADES

Despite Francis Thompson expressing a determined desire to switch careers from poetry to journalism, following his return to London in 1897, instead he was soon back composing new verses. However, now his work was full of the romantic ardour of an earnest lover. The object of his affections being yet another of Wilfrid Meynell's poetic protégé's, a member of that closely-knit literary inner circle, Katherine Douglas King, invariably known as Katie. An aspiring writer herself, she had recently come to know and admire Thompson's work, beginning a correspondence with him, while he was away in North Wales working on the completion of his third volume of poetry.

The youngest of four children, Katie's father, Henry King, was originally a book seller in Brighton before moving into publishing alongside his brother-in-law, George Smith. Among their early successes was a first volume of poetry written by Alice Meynell. When the partnership was dissolved, Smith continued the publishing house, while King founded the firm of H.S. King and Co, East India bankers and agents with offices in London, Liverpool, Marseilles, Port Said, Bombay, Calcutta, Delhi and Simla. The company was eventually assimilated into Lloyd's Bank, King becoming a director. Following King's death in 1878, son, Seymour, took over the business, sharing the responsibility with that of being the longstanding Member of Parliament for Hull Central.

Katie's mother, Harriet Eleanor Hamilton King, who strongly and vehemently disapproved throughout of Thompson's relationship with Katie, was herself the daughter of a distinguished English admiral. She first met

Katie's father having submitted some work to Henry King's Cornhill office. Hugely impressed, after a brief courtship, the couple were later married. Notable among her subsequent output is *Aspromonte*, published in 1869, soon being followed by, *The Disciples, Letters and Recollections of Mazzini*, which went through ten editions. A convert to Catholicism, among her numerous religious tracts was *The Prophesy of Westminster, and other poems in honour of Henry Edward, Cardinal Manning*, published by Macmillan in 1895.

Appearing that same year was the first of Katie's five novels, *The Scripture Reader of Saint Mark's*, as she graphically outlines a saint's temptation and fall. This she followed with *Father Hilarion*, where her main character, The Honourable Hilarion Montalbert is a man who seeks relief from a remorseful past by serving in the Priory of the Sacred Heart, only to find that the defences which he has raised are powerless against human nature. Always using the pseudonym of K. Douglas King, whom many critics took to be man, *The Child Who Will Never Grow Old*, appeared in 1898, *A Bitter Vintage*, the following year and finally, in 1900, *Ursula*. She had also previously contributed a series of short stories to Wilfrid Meynell's *Merry England* magazine.

In February 1897, with Thompson now back in London, he received a letter from Katie. Uncomfortable with her mother's somewhat overbearing and interfering presence, she was keen to express her regret for what she described as the "unwarrantable and unnecessary" interference in their relationship and re-iterating her feeling that they may well have a future together. Though based in Chigwell, Katie had long been involved in charitable work in London's East End. There she worked in a hospital in Leonard Square, caring for disabled children. Here, signing her letter, Katherine Douglas King, she ends it with an invitation to Thompson to visit her and see the work she undertakes:

> I am a great deal at the little children's hospital. Mr Meynell knows the way. I Know that you are very busy now you are writing a great deal and your book is coming out, isn't it? But if you are able and care to come, you know how glad I shall be.
>
> Ever yours sincerely
>
> Katherine Douglas King

Happily accepting the invitation, meetings and letters duly followed as the relationship increasingly deepened. With Thompson still very much on the rebound after his very recent affair while in North Wales with Maggie

Brien, he was soon writing poems to Katie. Many have remained hidden from view within his numerous notebooks. In one, he makes mention that Katie has now firmly replaced Alice Meynell in his affections. Particularly notable among his public outburst of feelings were the five sonnets that had appeared in print under the collective title, *Ad Amicam*. Mrs King, as always conscious of her daughter's reputation, remained totally unimpressed, and was not slow to outline her feelings. In the interim, the poet had very publicly asked of Katie:

> O friend, who mak'st the mis-spent word of 'friend'
> Sweet as the low note that a summer dove
> Fondles in her warm throat! And shall it end
> Because so swift on friend and friend broke love?

Despite Mrs King's best efforts, four years of courtship seemed to be progressing well until the early months of 1900. Meanwhile, Katie, possibly at her mother's behest, had gone on a Dutch sailing holiday helping to crew her brother's yacht, *Heartsease*. While in Holland, it seems she met the Oxford educated, Reverend Edmund Godfrey Burr, the Vicar of Rushall in the West Midlands. She would soon write to Thompson;

Forest Hall
April 11,1900

My dear Francis

I have been wanting to write to you for so long; and now I find it a little difficult because one feels reluctant to speak of one's own great happiness to one whose life has been so sad and lonely as yours, even though that one should be so firm and true a friend as you have ever been to me. Perhaps you may have heard that I am engaged to be married to Mr Godfrey Burr, Vicar of Rushall near Walsall in Staffordshire; and our marriage is fixed for the early part of July. Although my new home will be far away we both hope that in time we may come to live nearer London, and I hope that my marriage will bring me not less but more in touch with my friends, amongst whom, Francis, I hope that I may ever count you as one of the first and nearest. Goodbye dear Francis, and may God bless you.

Your always affectionately
Katherine D. King

Godfrey Burr and Katie King were duly married at Woodford Parish Church a mere two months later. Given away by her mother, Katherine was attended by her sisters, Margaret, Lilian and Laura. Among the two hundred and fifty guests were the whole Meynell clan, including Olivia, who appeared as one of the pages. However, on 26th March, 1901, following the birth of twins, aged only thirty two, Katie tragically died, the result of puerperal fever.

A devastated Thompson, falling back into seclusion and drug addiction after losing Katie, poured his grief and despair into a sonnet that has long remained unpublished:

> So now, give o'er; for you are lost, I see,
> And this poor babe was dead even its birth,
> Which I had thought a young Joy born to me,
> Who had no child but Sorrow: and with mirth
> I gazed upon its face, nor knew it dead,
> And in my madness vowed that it did smile
> I said: 'Dear Soul, learn laughter, leave thy shed
> Sore tears, put off thy mourning weeds a while.
> This is our child a space, even though it die
> Hereafter; laugh a season, though it be
> Thy tears are but sad jewels thou put'st by,
> One day to wear again.' Very wan she
> Tried, doubting, unused smiles; then bowed her head:-
> Much, tears have made thee blind: this, too, is dead!'

Alongside this huge personal blow, came the further devastating news of the death of his long-time friend and confidante, Canon John Carroll who, since 1895, had been the Bishop of Shrewsbury. Returning to Staybridge for the Requiem Mass, Thompson slipped quietly in and out of the church, speaking to no one. Further disappointment came in the form of the publisher's rejection of the proposed fourth volume of his poetry. For Thompson, Carroll's death broke a last link with the past. Doing no work for six months, he quickly returned to his old habits of wandering the streets while, to blank out increasing illness, both real or imaginary, he resumed his drug habit. Meynell, practical as always, worked hard to fill his time and keep him busy with an ever increasing volume of work.

Throughout his many years in the capital, Thompson invariably took lodgings in North London, never very far from the Harrow Road, The Skiddaw Pub or the church of St Mary of the Angels in Bayswater. After his return from Wales, initially a house guest of his publisher, Arthur Doubleday in Whitehall Gardens, he then moved first to 39 Goldney Road, before lodging at 16 Elgin Avenue. However, after almost setting himself on fire by leaving a burning pipe in his pocket, not an unusual occurrence, he later moved close by to Number 28. He would live there for almost five years, the longest he ever occupied one dwelling since leaving home. While there, his landlady, printer's wife, Barbara Maries, like many before her, became his faithful, patient yet often puzzled friend, kept sweet and in pocket by the ever dutiful Wilfrid Meynell.

Another unfortunate mishap added further to his troubles during the winter of 1897. Wandering the streets totally oblivious to all and sundry, when crossing Holborn he was hospitalized having been knocked down by a passing hansom cab. The accident took place just as he was on his way to dine with Everard Feilding, a longstanding friend from his time spent at Pantasaph. As usual, never known for his time keeping, he arrived an hour late, but now with his head tied-up with a huge bandage. Knowing his past history, Feilding was immensely flattered that Thompson had even arrived at all. The two men would occasionally meet over the years, though Feilding increasingly felt that the poet was by now rapidly turning in on himself, more reclusive than ever before.

With his shyness rarely allowing anyone access to the window of his soul, Thompson did prove popular, most notably in the company of his fellow lodgers. On more than one occasion he even took part in a cricket outing with them. "I enjoyed it," he later told Everard Meynell, "though Bryant was dead on the stumps, hitting me with a trimmer on the kneecap, causing it to swell and later catching me on my left temple, the ball cannoning off a yard or two behind the stumps. My hat saved me!" Occupying another fourth floor room across the landing from Thompson was an Indian student named Sarath Kumar Ghosh. Soon after Thompson's death, Ghosh published his experiences in a novel entitled *The Prince of Destiny*. Here, Thompson retains his own name, while Barath is Ghosh himself:

> That night Barath was sleepless, the air was hot and oppressive. He arose and opened the window wide at the top. He looked at his watch and found it was past two o' clock. To let in some fresh air he also opened the door for a moment. And then stood still. Thompson's room was just opposite, across the corridor. Under the door Barath saw a thin line of light. A moment after it was obscured-just for a second, after which it was visible for seven seconds, and was again shut out. The occulation was repeated several times, almost with the same regularity. Thompson was slowly pacing up and down the room at that hour wrapped in thought.[1]

Surviving amid a regular diet of porridge and beer, in addition to The Skiddaw, his local pub at the corner of Elgin Avenue and Chippenham Road, there, from his regular seat next to the fire, he would watch the darts players and have his regular pork pie supper. His Sunday treat, if he could afford it, would invariably be roast beef followed by plum pudding. Thompson also frequented a small bar in Chancery Lane, The George Inn at Southwark, together with The Pillars of Wisdom in Greek Street, just off Soho Square. There he became friendly with the landlord, often whiling away the time in an evening of cigars, wine and often heated conversation, whether it be on cricket, religion or literary matters. Sadly, few who met him in these often destitute days, have left any form of description. One who did was a certain J.M. Stuart Young who, in an edition of *The Catholic World* of August, 1927, remembered Thompson thus:

> It was a misty day in November, the pavements were iridescent with London's most irksome slime. Thompson wore a frowzy Inverness cape; and the said cape was thrown back, thrust half aside to accommodate a fish basket, slung by leather straps over his shoulder.....He was not handsome; and yet there was a brilliancy in his restless eyes that arrested attention....his hands were noticeably artistic-long and white and plastic. On this occasion I drew him aside into the peace of Fountains Court.....we found a seat even while the sponge soft rain soaked our faces and our knees. Soon I persuaded him to talk to me about his visions. The slight moodiness that had shrouded his face vanished as if by magic; and he rhapsodised for an hour snuggled beneath my umbrella.[2]

Away from his lodgings, while researching for his volume on Saint Ignatius Loyola, Thompson regularly frequented the British Museum. Increasing indolence meant that the extended article would not be completed until a few months before his death. By now he was missing so many deadlines that, to get around this, the staff of *The Athenaeum* used to pretend that the paper was going to press some days earlier. Two curious melodramas, *Napoleon Judges: A Tragedy in Two Scenes* and a rather strange two-headed conversation piece, *Man Proposes, But Woman Disposes; Un Conte sans Raconteur*, date from this time, but for many years remained forgotten and unpublished.

Far more impressive though is one of his final works, *The Kingdom of God* or to give it its alternative title, *In No Strange Land*. Found later among his papers following his death, it has long puzzled scholars. Finished or not, unrevised or not, for many it remains one of Thompson's most perfect offerings, crowning his literary career with a vision he had sought for so long:

O world invisible, we view thee,
O world intangible, we touch thee,
O world unknowable, we know thee,
Inapprehensible, we clutch thee!

Does the fish soar to find the ocean,
The eagle plunge to find the air-
That we ask of the stars in motion
If they have rumour of thee there?

Not where the wheeling systems darken,
And our benumbed conceiving soars!-
The drift of pinions, would we hearken,
Beats at our own clay-shuttered doors.

The angels keep their ancient places;-
Turn but a stone, and start a wing!
'Tis ye, 'tis your estrangèd faces,
That miss the many-splendoured thing.

But (when so sad thou canst not sadder)
Cry;- and upon thy so sore loss
Shall shine the traffic of Jacob's ladder
Pitched betwixt Heaven and Charing Cross.

Yea, in the night, my Soul, my daughter,
Cry,- clinging Heaven by the hems;
And lo, Christ walking on the water
Not of Gennesareth, but Thames!

This late flowering from seeds sown during those many nights spent under the arches at Charing Cross undoubtedly passes way beyond the merely devotional and on to the mystical. One unintended consequence that no one could have foreseen, lies rather hidden within the poem's sixteenth line. Perhaps somewhat different from what the poet intended, that particular phrase would go on to inspire a book and a Hollywood film, with its title song by Sammy Fain and Paul Francis Webster, *Love Is a Many Splendored Thing*, winning an Academy Award in 1955 for the Best Original Song. This beautifully shot and emotive film, directed with such care by Henry King, was set in Hong Kong at the time of the Korean War. Starring William Holden and Jennifer Jones, it also won an Oscar for its costume designer, Charles Le Maire.

It was a poetry review that, in the autumn of 1898, first brought Thompson into contact with the English writer and poet, Wilfrid Scawen Blunt. A close friend of Wilfrid Meynell, passionately devoted to Arabian culture, this many-sided man of independent means had been impressed by Thompson's opinions on his verse and persuaded Wilfrid and Alice to bring him to his Sussex estate for a visit. Thompson, now free for a time of his drug addiction, but never completely at ease, made something of an impression on Blunt as he recorded in his diary:

> I met them at the station, a very lovely day, and as we drove through the woods, Meynell pointed out that the poet of nature was wholly absorbed in the Globe newspaper he had brought down with him in the train, such being the way with London poets. Thompson, though born in Lancashire and speaking English with a broad provincial accent, is a true Cockney. He is a little weak-eyed, red-nosed young man of the degenerate London type, with a complete absence of virility and a look of raptured dependence on Mrs Meynell which is most touching. He is very shy, but was able to talk a little when the conversation was not too loud, and he seems good-hearted and quite unpretending. He has written no poetry Meynell tells me, now for some years, being cured of his morphia. But Meynell thinks the fountain may someday break forth again. Meanwhile he gets a living by literary criticism in the Academy and other journals. When I went out after luncheon to the woods, I found him quite ignorant of the names of the commonest trees, even the elm, which he must have seen every day in London. On the whole I quite liked him, for he was quite simple and straightforward. Only it was difficult to think of him as capable of any kind of strength in rhyme or prose.[3]

With their extensive family by now scattered far and wide and with Meynell a director of Burns and Oates, in 1905, Wilfrid and his wife rented out Palace Court and moved to a flat spread over the third and fourth floors above the offices of his publishers at the corner of Granville Place and Oxford Street. When attending a supper there with her sister, Harriet Monroe later somewhat unkindly reflected on Francis Thompson as, "the most pathetic little figure of ruin I have ever seen, plain almost repellent with his ragged sandy beard, blotched skin and watery eyes, his blurred consciousness of us or anything going on."[4] By now both Alice and the children were also finding Thompson's unkempt appearance and lack of personal hygiene increasingly irksome.

Of those children, eldest daughter, Monica, long Thompson's favourite of the girls, had married in 1903, a doctor, Caleb Saleeby. Thompson, having been invited to the ceremony at St Mary of the Angels Church in Bayswater, but as was his wont, had got the time hopelessly wrong and missed the whole event. The poppy that she picked and gave him, with "Keep it as long as you live," was found in the leaves of his personal copy of *New Poems*, the only volume of poetry he ever kept with him. Suffering periodically from depression, she would later tragically take her own life. Olivia, also a writer, would wed Murray Sowerby, the couple settling in Bristol where her husband went on to become a Director of the Imperial Tobacco Company. In April 1907, Madeline married Percy Lucas, the younger brother of Thompson's literary friend and fellow cricket enthusiast, Edward Verrall Lucas. The couple would later have three daughters.

Viola, who in 1922 was based in Sussex, became Mrs John Dallyn, marrying the tenant of the neighbouring Manor Farm. A member of the Women's Emergency Corps during the Great War, among her extensive literary output, she compiled a fascinating memoir exploring the close relationship between Francis Thompson and Wilfrid Meynell.[5] A study of her mother, initially published in 1929, was reissued in 1947 to celebrate Alice's centenary.[6] Together with her brother, Francis and sisters, Monica and Olivia, in 1910, the quartet published *Eyes Of Youth: A Book of Verse*, featuring poetry by Padraic Colum, Shane Leslie, Viola Meynell, Ruth Lindsay, Hugh Austin, Judith Lytton, Olivia Meynell, Maurice Healy, Monica Saleeby, all interspersed with four early works by Francis Thompson.[7]

Among the boys, the youngest, Francis, educated at Downside and Trinity College, Dublin, was, like his mother and sisters, a vigorous supporter of the Suffragette Movement and, during the First World War, a prominent conscientious objector. Having helped found the Anglo Russian Democratic Alliance, he later worked as a journalist. Of his many and varied pursuits, smuggling diamonds out of Russia to help finance the *Daily Herald* newspaper was perhaps the most dramatic. Also, a noted poet and book designer, having founded the famed Nonesuch Press, he later worked as a highly successful advertising executive in the film industry. Married three times, he was knighted in 1946. Remaining very much in the background was the eldest son, Sebastian who, after an early career in journalism, then edited the *Catholic Who's Who* for a time, before going on to work closely alongside his father.

His brother, Everard, Francis Thompson's closest confidante, possibly understood the poet better than most. Indeed, he became one of Thompson's ablest biographers, the first edition of his thickly packed memoir being published in 1913.[8] Having studied at the Slade School of Art, he later specialised in art criticism. As a noted bibliophile and book seller, his Serendipity Shop, first in Westbourne Grove and later in Shepherd's Market, became a noted mecca for book enthusiasts. At the rear of the premises was a large art studio where the poet regularly sat for him. Having served in the Great War, Everard and his wife Grazia later spent some time in America. He died in 1926.

With Francis Thompson now increasingly overwhelmed by an impending sense of doom, not only for himself but for the world in general, now more than ever illnesses of every kind relentlessly bore down upon him. To try and cheer him up, Everard Meynell could never resist inviting Thompson to Lord's or the Oval to watch Lancashire play. Increasingly reluctant to accept, instead he preferred to dwell on his memories of yesteryear. Little could anyone at the time have realised that unleashing such a wave of nostalgia would ultimately contribute in no small part to the poet's immortality.

28 Elgin Avenue
Friday [22nd July, 1905]

Dear Everard,

I write to remind you I shall be at the shop to-morrow. I think despite my disappointments, I shall make a final effort to see Lancashire's second innings – though I know it will be a failure. I will try this time to get there before lunch – the third time pays for all, & I trust my third effort to get out early will succeed. I think it will.

Feet *etc.* worse again to-day; but the swelling never really goes, even when the pain does. I want to get to bed. Good night, with love to you all, especially the poor invalids.

Yours affectionally, dear Ev,
Francis Thompson

I did not go to Lord's. Could not get there before lunch; & getting a paper a Baker St., saw Lanc. had collapsed & Middes. were in again. So turned back without getting my ticket – luckily kept from another disappointing day.

The following week Thompson wrote again to Everard:

28 Elgin Avenue,
Wednesday [27th July, 1905]

Dear Everard,

I write to remind you of tomorrow. Thank you very much for leaving me supplies today. I was upset, having been up till four *a.m.* in an attempt to finish my book. I will not be so foolish to-night, & will get to the shop in good time. I was sorry to find Olivia worse. May the nurse bring her round.

Haven't Yorks. & Lancs. had a good time of it at Old Trafford? What about Brearley in the Tests *now*? Next comes Yorks. v. Lancs., & don't I wish I were there! One of the York eleven at the Oval said they were "getting ready for Lancashire" – remembering Whit Monday at Old Trafford; & the Lancs. comment on his saying is, "Wigs on the green! Hurroo!"

We shall be ironed out, Ev.!
Love to all.

Yours affectionately,
F. Thompson

As work progressed on the Loyola volume, an ever astute Wilfrid Meynell arranged for Thompson to be paid piecemeal for every three pages of the volume produced. For this The Serendipity Shop, close to his lodgings, served as both a depository and a treasury. Thus, faithfully during May, June, July and into August of 1905, Thompson would arrive daily at the shop and claim a shilling to buy himself breakfast, lunch and supper, not to mention his laudanum. With a new project on the go, a proposed compilation of his prose, Thompson purchased a new notebook and began work. He had also been commissioned to write an ode on his alma mater, Ushaw College, to commemorate its 100th anniversary that would take place in 1908. Sadly, however, such intense intellectual activity required energy that he did not now seem to possess.

Towards the end of 1905, as the poet's physical and emotional slide was quickly accelerating in a downward spiral, a worried Wilfrid Meynell felt that it was imperative to get him out of London to spend the winter months in the healthier climes of Sussex. It was there, on the recommendation of the neighbouring Franciscan monastery, that he lodged with the newly-married Ted Gravely and his wife, whose cooking he took great delight in. Thinking he was there for just a month, he undertook a commission to write a feature on the English Catholic martyrs. He did not however, stop taking laudanum, having it mailed to him by a chemist he knew on the Harrow Road. Though liked by his hosts, despite his surfeit of colds and influenza, however his way of life began to grate.

His habit of sleeping late in the morning and then calling for his breakfast or staying in his room for days on end and, in one case spending two weeks alone, all took their toll on the couple. Eventually agreeing to a more sociable way of life, while completing a number of reviews, he stayed at Crawley until spring, 1906. With Mrs Gravely expecting their first child, it was thought best that Thompson return to London. Back at Elgin Avenue, he resumed work on the Ignatius study. Towards the end of the year he moved lodgings for a final time to 128 Brondesbury Road in Kilburn where, amid a steep and narrow flight of stairs, he took a room on the top floor. It had a lovely view overlooking the many delights of the District Line.

By now, in the early months of 1907, under the double onslaught of tuberculosis and opium, Meynell was becoming increasingly concerned about Thompson's health. Somewhat against his will, on the 24th August, Thompson was sent by car to Caxton's Farm, the Sussex estate of Meynell's literary friend, Wilfrid Blunt. While there, as before, he had some six ounces of laudanum posted to him every day by his friendly local chemist. Staying at the home of Blunt's retainer, David Roberts and his wife, Blunt would call and collect him every day him for lunch. While there, Blunt's son-in-law, Neville Lytton, famously took the opportunity to paint Thompson's portrait. Only able to sit for the artist ten minutes at a time, by now worries about the poet's health gave everyone increasing cause for concern:

> We had become alarmed about him latterly, as since the weather began to break up, he has remained entirely indoors, shut in David's cottage with a big fire and the windows carefully closed, a bottle of laudanum, David tells me, and ill with diarrhoea. It reduced him to a skeleton. Meynell has sent a priest to see him, and I felt that any day he might go suddenly. He needs someone with him who can exercise control over him, but I doubt his living over Christmas. As an intellectual force he is already dead, and his poor body is dying too.[9]

Weighing little more than five stone, Thompson returned to London, accompanied by Everard Meynell on October 16th, "so weak he had to be helped into the carriage." A few weeks later, on 2nd November, thanks to the influence of Monica Meynell's then husband, Dr Caleb Saleeby, Thompson entered the Catholic hospital of Saint John and Saint Elizabeth in St John's Wood, initially to undergo further drug treatment. Tucked in his boots the nurses found numerous little packets of white powder. While there, it was an ever alert Saleeby who had the presence of mind to draw up a will for Thompson to sign. Thus, on 12th November, when witnessed by a fellow patient, Joseph Fevre, Thompson just about managed to trace his signature. The result remains perhaps the simplest ever document in the history of literature:

I leave absolutely my literary copyrights and papers, including my manuscripts and unpublished poems, to Wilfrid Meynell, of 4 Granville Place Mans W

Throughout those twelve days in hospital, with Wilfrid Meynell keeping a constant vigil at his bedside, the poet began drifting in and out of consciousness. He died peacefully at dawn on 13th November, 1907. He was aged just forty seven. Around his neck as always was the medal of the Blessed Virgin. Three days later, on the 16th November 1907, he was interred in the Catholic section of St Mary's Cemetery, Kensal Green, only a few hundred yards from the house in which he had completed *The Hound of Heaven*. Placed in his coffin were roses from Meredith's garden, duly inscribed, *A true Poet, one of the small band.* Attending at the graveside were a mere dozen mourners. They included Wilfrid and Alice Meynell, Everard and his wife, Grazia, together with his last landlady, Mrs Randle.

Above the poet's grave stands the monument erected by Wilfrid Meynell. It is a simple stone sarcophagus designed by the sculptor Eric Gill. On its top, slightly raised, and stretching the length and breadth of the slab, lies a cross, the symbol that reconciled all things in life and death for the poet. On one end is a crown of thorns intertwined with a wreath of laurel. At the other is an inscription:

FRANCIS THOMPSON
1859-1907
LOOK FOR ME IN THE NURSERIES OF HEAVEN

All Thompson's worldly goods were contained within a small tin box full of rubbish, that included countless broken pens and pipes, numerous unopened letters, a wickless spirit lamp, his beloved toy theatre, not forgetting countless penny note books and, of course, his poems. As in life, so in death, Wilfrid Meynell once again served his protégé with considerable aplomb, quickly recruiting his many and varied contacts to write sympathetic notices on the late poet. Thus, six days after Thompson's death, on November 19th, 1907, most of the London papers carried detailed obituaries, many, if not all, emanating from the same source. From now on, Meynell would never rest until Thompson was proclaimed the prince of poets.

Among the tributes, the distinguished writer, Wilfred Whitten, wrote extensively about the poet in the weeks following his death. This article appeared in the November edition of *T.P's Weekly*:

I first met Francis Thompson at *The Academy* office in Chancery Lane, in 1897, the year in which, with his *New Poems*, he took farewell of poetry and began, I fear, to look on life as so much dead lift, so much needless postscript to his finished epistle. From that year until 1902 my intimacy with him grew out of our relationship on The Academy, to which I was assistant editor under Mr Lewis Hind, and he a most valued and most erratic contributor. We gave Thompson as many books of theology, history, biography and, of course poetry as he cared to review. It was a usual thing in reading the proofs, for one of us to exclaim aloud on his splendid handling of a subject demanding the best literary knowledge and insight. Thompson came frequently to the office to receive books for review, and to bring in his copy. Every visit meant a talk which was never curtailed by Thompson. This singer, who soared to themes too dazzling for all but the rarest minds; this poet of the broken wing and the renounced lyre had not become moody or taciturn. At his best he was a fluent talker, who talked straight from his knowledge and convictions, yet for victory. He weighed his words and would not hurt a controversial fly. On great subjects he was slow or silent; on trifles he became grotesquely tedious. This dreamer seemed surprised into a kind of exhilaration at finding himself in contact with small realities. And when the fountains of memory would be broken up, or some quaint corner of his amor propre would be touched. He would explain nine times what was clear and talk about snuff or indigestion or the posting of a letter until the room swam around us.[10]

In the November edition of *The Dublin Review*, Alice Meynell eloquently recorded her thoughts:

Francis Thompson's friends were few, and such as survive him should take the occasion while it is given them to record him as a living poet; as a poet of the past he will have a nation, a literature, a language to record him, as a man he has not a score of women and men. When he died, many who for the first time heard his name, gave him, imitating one another, the name and fame of a type of outcast or minor criminal. Perhaps the tragic tone of much of his poetry, forbidding the conjecture of jovial sin, yet suggested that of long remorse. But he was a man of singular innocence; he had what some schools of Christians place at the forefront of the Christian life – a 'conviction of sin'; nothing that concerns the world or its judgements. But he was not singularly, or often, unhappy. He had told all readers with a perfect freedom of communication all his own, what was the deprivation and the chief distress of his life. It is the deprivation that is the equally noble privilege of many thousands of women in our present civilisation; without avowal even to themselves they endure the lack of love that is between man and woman. The avowal made in his whole poetry by this solitary man implied no lapse in dignity.[11]

Wilfrid Meynell would pay his own hugely heartfelt tribute to the poet:

> Let none be named the benefactor of him who gave to all more than any could give to him. He made all men his debtors, leaving to those who loved him the memory of his personality and to English poetry an imperishable name.[12]

Nowhere was there a greater sense of pride in Francis Thompson's achievements than in his birthplace of Preston in Lancashire. It was soon home to a thriving Francis Thompson Appreciation Society that lasted well into the inter war years. There also, in 1912, came the publication of the poet's first biography. Entitled *Francis Thompson, The Preston Born Poet (with Notes on some of his works)*, it was compiled by local antiquarian and enthusiast, John Thomson, who at that time lived at 44 Avenham Street, close to the former Thompson family home. Published by public subscription, it opens with the following eloquent tribute - Thomson on Thompson[13]:

> Thompson, thy music like a deep stream flows
> From mystic heights, and mirrors as it goes
> The shades and splendours of that luring peak,
> Where poet-dreamers dwell, and tireless seek
> Their adequate strains; and thy song is fed
> By cyclic hauntings from the cliffs of dread
> Thou perforce clomb, a wider world to scan,
> And catch lost echoes of the Pipes of Pan.
>
> From other sounds aloof thy music rolls,
> And men *must* hearken for it draws their souls:
> Now thrills with awe, and now with such sweet stress
> As linketh heart to heart in tenderness
> By dire compellings, none save those may wield,
> Whose birth-fused breath is fashioned for the yield-
> Who reach the crownèd gates, and entrance gain
> To highest Heaven, through the arch of Pain!

Forty years later, Viola Meynell would examine the relationship of the poet with her father in her highly personal account, *Francis Thompson and Wilfrid Meynell: A Memoir*. Dedicated to her brother Sebastian, there she was able to draw on letters preserved by her father, few of which had ever been published, as she herself commented, "memory supplies much else." It was a story of two men who met in rather strange circumstances, lived totally different lives, and yet shared a common bond. In the interim had appeared Everard Meynell's extensive yet finely-drawn, *The Life of Francis Thompson*, which did much to sustain the poet's reputation. Here Everard writes of Thompson's final hours:

> But, for all that friends were at hand, the nurse tender, and the priest punctual, his passing was solitary.....The fires quenched were his own. It seemed to his friends as if it were a matter personal to himself, while their sorrow for their own loss was mixed almost with satisfaction at something ended in his favour, or at least he had had his way in a transaction with a Second Party, who might have long and painfully delayed the issue.......
>
> His features when I went to make a drawing of him in the small mortuary that stood among the wintry garden-trees, were entirely peaceful, so that I who had sometimes known them otherwise, fell into the mood of the cheerful lay-sister with the keys, who said, "I hear he had a very good death," To the priest who had seen him in communion with the church and her saints at the moment which may be accounted the most solitary possible to the heart of the man, no though of especial loneliness was associated with his death.

Having so skilfully and successfully orchestrated Thompson's numerous obituaries that appeared in all manner of varied publications, now as the poet's literary executor, Wilfrid Meynell was also perfectly placed to exploit the sudden explosion of interest that duly followed. Having found the essay on *Shelley*, rejected some eighteen years earlier by *The Dublin Review*, Meynell sent it again to the magazine, this time with hugely positive results. Its immediate success was quickly followed by an edition of *Selected Poems by Francis Thompson*, published in 1908, Meynell's judicious choice that included many of the poet's finest works. Over the next couple of years, this one volume alone, would sell well in excess of 20,000 copies.

While the biography of *St Ignatius Loyola* passed quietly, the three volumes of *The Works of Francis Thompson*, judiciously mixing poetry and prose, issued five years later, undoubtedly became the highpoint of Wilfrid Meynell's astute stewardship. Of Thompson's two hundred and fifty poems that eventually appeared in print, surprisingly only half had been published during his lifetime. By now however, with storm clouds gathering throughout Europe, the poet's popularity, was fast approaching its zenith. Following the Great War of 1914-18, attitudes had changed for ever and, save for the possible exception of *The Hound of Heaven* and *At Lord's*, Thompson's work never again quite commanded such unbridled adulation.

As literary executor, such large sales of Thompson's work invariably brought Wilfrid Meynell riches beyond his wildest dreams. Though still himself in constant demand as a writer, now he could afford to pick and choose his commissions. In 1941, sale of the original manuscript for *The Hound of Heaven* alone, brought in £1,000. It was Francis Meynell who once commented that the initial outlay on Francis Thompson had been repaid "many times over," and that he had been, "the richest of investments." However, Meynell's own volumes of verse, particularly *Aunt Sarah and the War*, published in 1915, *Who Goes There* and *Rhymes with Reason*, also earned him extensive royalties. This latter volume he dedicated to his son-in-law Percy Lucas who had been killed at the Battle of the Somme. Struck in the legs by two machine gun bullets, he died in hospital on 1st July, 1916, as complications set in. Beneath the dedication Meynell added the lines:

> I remember thee while the light lasts;
> And in the darkness I do not forget.

The vast bulk of Thompson's papers and notebooks, together with the libraries of publisher, John Lane and editor, Lewis Hind, were eventually purchased by an American poetry enthusiast, Seymour Adelman, who later donated his collection to Boston College, Chestnut Hill in Massachusetts. They comprise two hundred and ninety seven manuscripts, of which two hundred and forty six are poetry and fifty one are prose, together with one hundred and twenty one notebooks. There, for many years, they were faithfully curated by its librarian, Father Terence Connolly. In 1938, he came to England to spend almost four months following in Francis Thompson's footsteps to research a volume he entitled, *Francis Thompson, In His Paths.*[15] It was Connolly too, who, in 1957, added copiously to the Thompson canon, publishing *The Man Has Wings.*[16] It contained seventy four new poems and the two playlets, each one Connolly carefully assembling from the numerous earlier rough drafts now in his care.

Having returned to Boston from his highly rewarding trip to England, the many gifts Connolly collected, particularly from Wilfrid Meynell and others, were catalogued and added to the permanent collection of Thompson literature that is held at the College. With its high vaulted ceiling, stained glass windows The Thompson Room, dedicated to the poet's memory, is situated beneath the Gothic tower at the end of the Great Hall of the college library. Nowadays, the original manuscripts are stored in more secure and climate-controlled areas of the John J. Burns Library of Rare Books. Above the display cases are portraits of Wilfrid Meynell and his wife, Alice. On the opposite wall, in the centre, a facsimile of Raphael's *Granduca Madonna.* On the left of this is Thompson's exegete, Coventry Patmore. On the right, Francis Thompson himself.

During his visit to this country, Connolly visited Ushaw, delighting in finding over the fireplace in what was then the College Reading Room, Francis Thompson's memory being honoured by an elegant brass plaque. Today, though no longer a seminary, that same brass plaque remains in what has now become The Francis Thompson Lounge. A similar memorial, mounted on Hopton Wood marble, resides in the Harris Art Gallery and Museum in the poet's home town of Preston. Nearby, high on the wall of the poet's birthplace is the first ever tribute to the poet. Initially erected in 1910, it was the gift of Mrs Catherine Holliday. Today rather weather-worn, in common with Everard Meynell's autobiography, Thompson's date of birth remains incorrect.

1859 FRANCIS THOMPSON 1907
POET
WAS BORN IN THIS
HOUSE DEC. 16, 1859

"Ever and anon a trumpet sounds
From the hid battlements of Eternity"

While Preston itself, in 1913, had given birth to an initial somewhat highly localised Francis Thompson Society, it would be another half century before anything evolved on a more national scale. Driven forward by its founding Secretary, the then Hampstead based academic, Dr Gutala Krishnamurti, its Chairman was John Elkin. Serving as President was the often controversial creator of *Tarka the Otter*, writer, Henry Williamson. Its aim was to bring admirers of Thompson's work into an association and eventually acquire a building associated with the poet to establish a Francis Thompson Memorial Centre and Museum. Adding an international flavour to the organisation as Vice Presidents were the French scholar, Pierre Danchin and American author and Thompson biographer, Paul van Kuykendall Thomson, Associate Professor of English at Providence College, Rhode Island in the United States. However, save for a single commemorative exhibition and booklet, the organisation appeared to achieve little, eventually, in 1973, re-inventing itself for a brief period as the Eighteen Nineties Society.

Having settled happily in Thakeham, close to Storrington in Sussex, it was Monica and her husband, Percy Lucas, who first alerted Wilfrid Meynell and his wife to the many delights of country living. Up for sale was a small country house with eighty acres of common and woodland situated at Greatham, just three miles from their home. Immediately taken with both the locality and the property, Meynell bought the whole estate for little more than £20 an acre. A library was invariably added to the main house called Humphry's Homestead, while alterations and improvements were made to the numerous other outbuildings on the estate. Ultimately, Meynell would divide-up parts of the land for his children, so that, in due course, they could all build individual homes for themselves and their families.

Dotted at irregular intervals inside the surrounding stone walls were four giant poplar trees, all that was left of the original twelve originally planted there in honour of the Apostles. Later, close by the house stood a mock grave of Meynell's much mourned son-in-law, Percy Lucas. At its head, the white wooden cross that once marked his resting place in France. At its foot, a tall cypress bush, planted by Alice Meynell, originally a cutting taken from the tree on Shelley's grave. It was to this estate, particularly to Viola Meynell's home, the converted cow barn, later known as Shed Hall, that the writer D.H. Lawrence would come to work on novels such as, *The Rainbow*. For many years, until the writer cruelly abused the Meynell's hospitality, Viola would regularly type out his manuscripts for him.

Indeed it was Viola who, in 1946, hosted an impressive series of radio documentaries on major literary figures, that included her mother, Vita Sackville West, Ruth Pitter and Francis Thompson. Later that year, Viola and her brother, Francis, collaborated on a radio programme entitled *Return Journey*, in which they recalled in some detail their early years together at Palace Court. Fourteen years later, in June 1960, Francis himself took part in a belated centenary tribute to the poet on BBC Radio. His personal memories of Thompson were interspersed with poetry, the programme's two readers being the well-known actor, Valentine Dyall and a young up and coming Welsh poet named Dylan Thomas.

Earlier, a play written by an English journalist, Jack de Leon, was staged in London in 1933. A second, *Song out of Sorrow*, written by Felix Doherty, was produced in New York City in 1941. Here, occasional programmes on both radio and television have drawn attention both to the poet and his work. Among these was a 1978 radio play starring Robert Powell. Patric Dickinson's study, ten years later, was entitled *A Ladder Without Rungs*. Some years earlier in 1969, in *Mirror to an Age*, a programme made by Thames Television, presenter Bernard Keefe judiciously wove a narrative that mixed aspects of Edward Elgar's music with excerpts from Francis Thompson's poetry.

Remaining as industrious as ever was Meynell's wife, Alice. In 1913, a selection of her *Collected Poems* was published to great acclaim by Burns and Oates. A volume of her *Collected Essays* duly followed twelve months later. Elected President of the Society of Women Journalists, she was twice nominated for the post of Poet Laureate. Once, in 1895, proposed as a successor to Tennyson, and again, eighteen years later, following the death of Alfred Austin. Working on steadily helping her husband recreate much of Thompson's unpublished poetry, increasing heart trouble sadly dogged her later years. She died, aged 75, on November 27th 1922, and, like Francis Thompson, she too is buried close by in the Catholic section of St Mary's Cemetery, Kensal Green.[17]

Adjoining the flat grey slab that delineates Alice's grave stands a large bronze figure of the Crucified. The bowed head of the dying Christ here looking down on the last resting place of another of Wilfrid Meynell's literary protégés, the renowned Irish novelist and poet, Katharine Tynan. It was her poetry that inspired Francis Thompson's *The Sere of the Leaf*, written at the end of 1890 and first published in *Merry England* in January 1891. Alongside her own prolific output of poetry and prose, she also became an articulate advocate of Thompson's work, as witnessed by her very fine appreciation published in *The Fortnightly Review* in 1910. For all the undoubted exasperation he invariably engendered, she remembered him with particularly warm affection:

> There was something loveable about him, about his simplicity, his humanity, his humbleness, which perhaps made the burden of his faithful friends lighter, as it made their grief heavier when he died.[18]

At the time of his wife's death, Wilfrid Meynell was aged seventy. Despite becoming increasingly infirm however, thanks to family support over the next quarter of a century, he was able to continue to split his time between Palace Court in London and his Sussex country estate. There, proving particularly active in his role of venerable elder statesman, he made that part of Sussex, near to Parham Woods, a legendary haunt of English letters. Awarded a C.B.E. in 1943, he died, aged 96, on the 20 October, 1948. Happy to sacrifice his own muse to others, this patriarch of English Catholic writers gave unsparingly of his time and talent to nurture countless young literary hopefuls aspire to greatness. However, no matter how hard he tried, he never did quite find another Francis Thompson.

There can be no question that, particularly for Wilfrid Meynell, Francis Thompson, as the prince of poets, made both English poetry and prose come alive. Likewise, Gerald Manley Hopkins, believed him a genius born before his time. It is also timely perhaps to recall G.K. Chesterton's comment on the poet in *The Victorian Age in Literature*:

> None of the Victorians were able to understand Francis Thompson; his sky-scraping humility, his mountains of mystical detail, his occasional and unashamed weakness, his sudden and sacred blasphemies. Perhaps the shortest definition of the Victorian Age is that he lived outside it.[19]

For many others however, Francis Thompson has been a complex and often controversial character, somewhat elusive, perhaps too incorporeal ever to be a truly major figure. Despite this, he remains a fine and sincere craftsman with a genuine creative spark and moments of deep vision, who undoubtedly made a valuable contribution to the life of his own generation. Often or not such work is sadly forgotten for a time until subsequent consideration reminds us just how good the very best of it truly was.

Writing more than half a century ago, the poet's devoted godson, Sir Francis Meynell, was forced by circumstance to ask – "What best represents Thompson's genius?" After some considerable thought, he went on, "I think everyone will find what the distinguished critic, J.L. Garvin found: " his poems swarm in our ears like bees."[20]

A phrase of the poet's that swarms with many others in my own head is this;

Lo, God's two worlds immense
Of spirit and of sense
Wed
In this narrow bed

Time itself is a very narrow bed and what governed the heart say forty, fifty or even sixty years ago, is not necessarily what moves it today. But the poetry of Francis Thompson, the poetry of spirit and of sense, will surely continue to obey for many generations his own distinct injunction:

Song, turn on thy hinge again.

Appendix I

O My Hornby And My Barlow Long Ago!

It is little I repair to the matches of the Southron folk,
        Though my own red roses there may blow;
It is little I repair to the matches of the Southron folk,
        Though the red roses crest the caps I know.
For the field is full of shades as I near the shadowy coast,
And a ghostly batsman plays to the bowling of a ghost,
And I look through my tears on a soundless clapping host,
        As the run-stealers flicker to and fro,
                To and fro:-
        O my Hornby and my Barlow long ago!

This single set of ten lines was initially published by Wilfrid Meynell in *The Athenaeum* of November 1907, as part of a tribute following the poet's death. Twelve months later, in an article outlining Francis Thompson's extensive cricket writings, Edward Verrall Lucas published the poem in full in *The Cornhill Magazine.*[1] Although not titled, as now, the poem consisted of four stanzas, the last being a repeat of the opening. Twelve months later, this article was republished in his subsequent book, *One Day and Another*, but now entitled, *A Rhapsodist at Lord's*. Such a title has, in some later editions, been attributed to the poem itself. However, in Wilfrid Meynell's 1913 publication, *The Collected Poetical Works of Francis Thompson*, the original single stanza was simply headed, *At Lord's*.

Within other collections of the poet's work, a small number of different variations have also appeared. In Clement Shorter's edition of T*he Uncollected Verses by Francis Thompson*, privately printed in 1917, the following stanza was given:

For the field is full of shades/shadows as I near the shadowy coasts,
And the ghostly batsmen play, and the bowlers too are ghosts,
And the ghostly batsmen play to the bowling of the ghosts,
And the ghostly batsmen play silent balls of bowling ghosts,
And I see the ghostly batsmen that play to bowling ghosts,
And I look through my tears at a soundless clapping/cheering host
As/While/Where the run-stealers flicker to and fro,
        To and fro.
O my Hornby and my Barlow long ago!

Yet another little-known verse was quoted independently from the rest of the work by Everard Meynell in his article, *The Notebooks of Francis Thompson*, which first appeared in *The Dublin Review* of January 1917. Here Meynell perceptively notes: Thompson's cricket verses were all lamentations for the dead, the poet never happier than when mourning his heroes.

Somewhere still ye bide among my long-lost Northern faces,
My heroes of the past, they tell me so!
Somewhere still ye bide in my long-lost Northern places,
But dead to me with youth, long ago.
I mind me of your staunchness as I near the shadowy water,
O Stonewall, and the look of your little fair-haired daughter;
(But the years have done upon you all the unassuagable slaughter)
As the run-stealers flicker to and fro,
        To and fro,
O my Monkey and my Stonewall long ago!

In 2001, when Thompson's biographer, Brigid Boardman published her extensive and definitive edition of Thompson's poetry, she also included this verse as the fourth stanza of the poem and titled the whole work, *A Rhapsodist at Lord's*.[2]

The match that lies at the work's very heart, Lancashire versus Gloucestershire, took place at Old Trafford on July 25-27th, 1878. It was a historic contest, for the two counties had never met before. The fame of the three Graces, not merely the legendary William Gilbert Grace but his brothers, Edward and George, was such that 16,000 people were present on the Saturday when it is thought that a further 2,000 entered for free. Altogether some 28,000 spectators, including Francis Thompson, were reckoned to have seen the match. Doing much for the home county's cricketing prestige as well as its finances, the gate alone realised a remarkable £750. Sprinkling stardust as they went, the Grace family, aided by Francis Thompson's lines, helped county cricket move into a much more modern age.

Overall, amid interruptions for the weather, it was very much Hornby and Barlow's match. In the first innings, Hornby made only five, while Barlow, as was usual, batted right the way through for a solid 40. Not to be outdone, in the second innings Hornby was back to his ebullient best, making yet another magnificent 100. Barlow ended up with 80. For Gloucestershire, E.M. Grace made 21 and 4, also taking four wickets, as did his illustrious brother. Indeed, W.G.'s 58 not out in the second innings went a long way to ensuring the match ended as a draw, the visitor's finishing the game on 111 for five. Not celebrated in the haunting ode was the fact that Hornby, not for the last time in his illustrious career, upset by a number of malcontents, dived into the crowd and made a dramatic citizen's arrest.

However, had it not been for the sportsmanship of W.G., early in William Patterson's innings, the outcome might have been very different. The umpire, not seeing if one of Patterson's drive had crossed the boundary did not signal four. But, in the meantime, hearing the shouts from the crowd, the batsmen stopped running and Patterson's wicket was put down. After an objection was raised, the two captains held a long consultation, with Dr Grace (E.M. aka the Coroner) going into the crowd to speak to the spectators. When it was confirmed that the ball had indeed crossed the boundary, Patterson was allowed to continue his innings. Ironically, thanks to that bit of good fortune, he went on to record his only half century for the county, the highest score of his eight year Lancashire career.[3]

Thompson's countless shabby notebooks remained the poet's constant companions throughout his somewhat short creative journey. Whenever he moved lodgings they continued to be the only possessions that stayed with him. Everything else he would happily discard or sell. Verbally inventive, any idea would be instantly jotted down and then later corrected or discarded as a work evolved. There are often five or six variants for a single word. To say that he chose carefully and with purpose is not, of course to say that he always chose well. Lines such as:

O my Hornby and my Barlow long ago!

At one point Thompson's jottings show him seriously considering another alternative;

O My Monkey and Stone-waller long ago!

Monkey, as Thompson very well knew was, of course, A.N. Hornby's nickname from his school days at Harrow. At a mere 5ft 3ins tall, somewhat swarthy in looks and weighing - even with a bat in his hand - barely six and a half stone, he was an utterly fearless pocket dynamo. Once assigned, the soubriquet never left him. One of the biggest personalities the world of sport has ever produced, countless tales abounded about his many and varied exploits. While most were undoubtedly true, those that turned out to be apocryphal were often true in spirit. Throughout his life, thanks to the substantial family fortune, he remained the archetypal amateur Corinthian. Both Hornby and A.E. Stoddart remain the only sportsmen to have captained their country at both cricket and rugby union.

One of a family of eleven, seven boys and four girls, Albert Neilson Hornby was born in Blackburn on 10th February 1847. His father, William Henry Hornby was the first mayor of Blackburn who, for twelve years, from 1857 until 1869, represented the constituency in parliament. As the owners of Brookhouse Mill, the family's extensive wealth came from the Lancashire cotton industry. Educated, like his brothers at Harrow School, while his academic record there was undistinguished, he soon found cricketing success. In 1864, using an undersized bat, he famously helped the school to victory in the annual encounter with Eton at Lord's. He later moved seamlessly to Oxford University, but on discovering that as well as playing sport he was expected to study, he left in haste without a degree.

Marrying Ada Sarah Ingram, the daughter of a Lincolnshire Member of Parliament and founder of *The Illustrated London News* in 1876, the couple went on to have four sons, Albert, Walter, George and John. Living initially at Bridge House at Church Minshull in Cheshire, they later moved to the impressive 16 room stone colonnaded Parkfield House, close to his parents in the historic market town of Nantwich, some three miles west of Crewe. Revelling in his life as a country squire, amid his picturesque twenty-eight-acre estate, Hornby built a cricket pitch, ran his own beagle pack and stabled an impressive array of horses. Both he and his wife played a dominant role in the affairs of the Cheshire Hunt. He rode, it was said, with the same uncomplicated verve he displayed at the crease.

Of the couple's four children, all educated like their father at Harrow, two chose the military option, one dying in South Africa, the other perishing in the 1914-18 War. The eldest, Albert Henry, born in 1877, would follow in his father's footsteps as a sporting gentleman, later succeeding Archie MacLaren as Captain of Lancashire. Second son, Walter Ingram, born twelve months later, became an Australian sheep farmer. He later served as a Private in the 32nd Australian Infantry, one of the first Antipodean contingents to land in France. He died in Oxford just a week before the end of the Great War, of wounds received in combat, and is buried with his father. Their third child,

George, a member of the South African Constabulary, served in the Boer War and died in 1905, aged only 26.

Born in 1880, youngest son Jack, totally rejected the comfort and privilege of his background. Having failed to gain entry to the Diplomatic Service in 1904, he left Nantwich for Canada and the life of a gentleman adventurer. During the Great War, he was gassed at Ypres and wounded at the Somme, his gallantry winning him a Military Cross. Back in Canada, hailed as *The Hermit of the North*, he canoed to the uninhabited eastern end of the Great Slave Lake, built himself a cabin and survived alone through two of the coldest winters on record. A later expedition ended tragically when he and two companions died of starvation, their bodies eventually being found in 1929. The subject of numerous articles, books and plays, today Hornby Point and Hornby Fort proudly bear his name.

As a cricketer, invariably playing bare-headed, Hornby Senior was a bustling and dashing right hand batsman with a vast appetite for runs. Initially integrated into the Lancashire middle order, he later found fame opening the innings. While not a big man, aided by deft footwork, he proved a natural stroke player ideally suited both in style and temperament to dominate any attack from the very outset of his innings. However, throughout his career, he remained a highly over optimistic judge of a run. It was said that he had run his entire side out once and to have gone halfway to doing so a second time. His fielding, mostly in the covers was certainly on a par with his batting. He could also bowl and take wickets, with his occasional off spin, both right or left handed, depending on his mood.

Having completed his education, Hornby subsequently honed his cricketing talents, alongside his father and brothers, with the East Lancashire club at the newly opened Alexandra Meadows ground. Quickly making his mark, against Accrington in 1870 he remained undefeated with a chanceless 214. Three years earlier, he had made his first class debut batting down the order for Lancashire against Yorkshire at neighbouring Whalley. Between then and 1874, he would appear somewhat intermittently for the county. In the interim, having starred for the Gentlemen against the Players at Lord's in 1872, in the illustrious company of W.G. Grace and Lord Harris, later that year Hornby was selected as a member of R.A. Fitzgerald's team that made an extensive tour of North America.

An equally dashing wing three quarter, having played his club rugby for Preston Grasshoppers and Manchester prior to representing Lancashire, Hornby was aged thirty when he was first capped by England. Making his debut as they beat Ireland by two goals and two tries at the Oval in February 1877, two years later he was in the England side that competed in the inaugural Calcutta Cup game against Scotland. Winning his ninth and final cap in 1892, that year he captained England as they lost by two tries to nil against Scotland at Whalley Range in Manchester. He later served on the Rugby Football Union. As an athlete, he proved no less adept as a sprinter and hurdler. Likewise, both as a billiards player and as a boxer, he never missed an opportunity to take on all-comers just for fun of it.

An equally fine soccer player, Hornby first played for Blackburn Rovers when they beat Partick Thistle 2-1 at Alexandra Meadows in January 1878. He later played for his local team, Nantwich Town. Earlier, before the rules were codified, he had also run his own invitation side who played the game under the then rather strange Eton and Harrow rules, something of hybrid mixture of both rugby and soccer. He would later become President of the Lancashire Football Association. A good shot, he served as a Major in the East Cheshire Militia, spending a month prior to every cricket season assiduously training with the regiment. When hosting regular shooting parties at the nearby Dorfold Hall Estate, he would then donate the resulting presents of game and wildfowl to the sick and poor throughout the locality.

This pocket Hercules succeeded Edmund Rowley as Lancashire captain in 1880. A total autocrat, famously dubbed *The Boss*, and ruling Old Trafford somewhat imperiously, he soon proved to be one of the most astute leaders of his era creating a team of close friends: happy in success, united in adversity. Of course, he had a strong hand to play. His main bowlers, Crossland and Nash, while undoubtedly controversial, were certainly the most feared attack on any kind of wicket. The batting, if not comparable, gave him enough runs to play with. Supporting everyone behind the stumps was that *Prince of Wicket Keepers*, Richard Pilling. As always, driving Hornby on was the elemental proposition that matches were meant to be won and that every ball was destined for punishment.

1881 would prove to be a season of triumph for both Hornby and the county as, for the very first time, they clinched the coveted county championship title. Unbeaten in thirteen encounters, six of their wins were obtained with an innings to spare. To a large degree they also dominated their three drawn matches. For Hornby, the cares of captaincy certainly did little to inhibit his profligacy with the bat. Amassing 1,002 runs at an average of 50.02, his three centuries included the highest score of his career, 188, made against Derbyshire at Old Trafford. Further centuries followed against Kent, and the return encounter with Derbyshire. He undoubtedly had more than a fair claim to be the batsman of the year, even surpassing the exploits of his old adversary, the legendary William Gilbert Grace.

As a cricketer, Hornby never lost the aggressiveness of the small man. Any criticism, whether by individuals or groups, would be strongly challenged. During one match at Old Trafford he rushed up the 43 steps of the old Press Box, seized one unfortunate reporter by the collar, and frogmarched him out of the ground. Amid a pitch invasion when in Australia in 1879, as Lord Harris was being attacked, Hornby apprehended the main offenders. Despite being struck in the face and having his shirt torn, he successfully rounded them all up, marched them to the pavilion, and passed them into the arms of the law. He had the final satisfaction of seeing them charged in court. Once, when one of his sons was being loudly barracked, Hornby Senior held up the game to give the heckler a piece of his mind.

Despite thriving on confrontation, there were also numerous examples of his kindness and understanding. One such instance took place at Old Trafford in June 1884, when Gloucestershire were once again the visitors. W.G. Grace was in the pavilion waiting to bat when he received an urgent telegram. Opening it, he learned that his mother had just died unexpectedly. Going out to bat, having scored a single, somewhat distressed, he confided in Hornby the sad news. In typical style, the Lancashire captain ordered that the game be immediately abandoned. As W.G., together with his brother E.M. and cousin Walter Gilbert, hurried off to catch a train back to Bristol, Hornby ensured that messages were sent all around the ground to inform the spectators of the tragic news.

Having comfortably passed 1,000 runs in 1881, Hornby repeated the feat the following year, ending the season having amassed 1,383 runs, the county sharing the championship with Nottinghamshire. That year his centuries included 121 not out, made for MCC in the second innings of their encounter with Cambridge University at Lord's. Always relishing the ambience at headquarters, he followed this with a superb 131 for Lancashire away to Middlesex. It was also at Lord's, when playing for MCC, during their game against Derbyshire in 1885, that he was credited with a hit for eight, four coming from an overthrow. Such was his fame that A.N. Norman, the *nom de plume* of Manchester composer Alfred Normanton, created a popular new piece for piano in his honour, *The Hornby Schottische*.[4]

In all, Hornby played three times for England, captaining his country twice. Having toured Australia with Lord Harris's side in 1878/9, he first captained England in the famous Ashes test at the Oval three years later. Such was the excitement that one spectator, George Spendlove, dropped dead and another gnawed through the handle of his umbrella: one batsman went in literally speechless; and another could not bowl until he had been fortified with champagne. England, set to make only 85 runs to win were undone by the magic of Hornby's nemesis, Australia's demon bowler, Tom Spofforth, losing by seven runs. Within a few days, a young journalist, Reginald Brooks, seemed to encapsulate the national mood when in *The Sporting Times* he published the following notice:

In affectionate Remembrance of
ENGLISH CRICKET
Which died at the Oval on
29th August 1882
Deeply lamented by a large
circle of Sorrowing Friends
and Acquaintances
R.I.P.
N.B. The body will be cremated
And the Ashes taken to Australia

One further test appearance followed when, two years later, along with team mates Barlow, Steel and Pilling, Hornby captained England in the drawn encounter against Australia at Old Trafford. Losing the first day to rain meant that this, the historic first ever test match played on home turf, petered out to a tame draw. Somewhat controversially, Hornby had appointed himself as captain, a decision that met with less than universal approval. His record as leader was poor - one defeat and one draw in his two matches in charge. He had also failed to do himself justice with the bat. Unable to reach double figures, he scored two and four in the Melbourne test, two and one at the Oval and four in front of his home crowd at Old Trafford, a miserable total of 21 runs at an average of 3.5.

Sharing the Lancashire captaincy with Sydney Crosfield in 1892 and 1893, Hornby was back in sole charge again in 1897, just in time to claim a second county championship title. His final appearance came two years later, some 32 years after his debut, when captained by his son and batting well down the order, he hit 53 against Leicestershire. Making some 292 appearances for the county, he totalled 10,694 runs with a top score of 188. He scored ten centuries. Never less than wholehearted and committed team player he also had 217 catches to his name. In all first class cricket, between 1867 and 1906, his 16,109 runs included 16 centuries and 313 catches. Two championship titles during his time as captain, not only points to the strength of the side, but also to the flair of the man who led it.

By now, having succeeded Sir Humphrey De Trafford as County President, Hornby served in that role until 1916. In at the birth of the club in 1864, over the ensuing half century, both on and off the field, he remained a dominant force. Against much initial opposition, as President, he oversaw the bold purchase of the ground and adjoining land for £25,000. He then proceeded to improve the facilities, most notably replacing the old and sparse wooden structures with much more modern buildings, including the magnificent new pavilion built in 1895 for £12,000. Very much a talismanic figure, rarely missing a game, he was the kind of long-serving hero any county would love to have. Luckily for Lancashire it was at Old Trafford that he chose to make such a big impression and leave his mark.

While revelling in his many roles on the national stage, not least a period as Joint Master of the Muskberry Hunt in County Cork, both Hornby and his wife also played a leading role in local affairs. A magistrate and Chairman of Crewe Divisional Conservative Association, for twelve years he represented the locality as a member of Cheshire County Council. He also helped oversee the management of the historic Beam Heath Trust. As a former player for his local cricket team, on becoming their President in 1897, he did much to help the club develop and improve the facilities at their Kingsley Fields ground. In 1904 it was strongly rumoured that he would soon be standing for Parliament as one of Blackburn's two M.P.'s, however he later withdrew his nomination.

Confined to a bath chair in later life, following injuries he sustained when a horse fell on him during a hunting trip, Hornby died from a heart attack, aged 78, on 17th December 1925. Amid much pomp and ceremony, he was buried in nearby Acton churchyard, alongside his second son, Walter Ingram Hornby. Just as he was being laid to rest, and while Thompson's poem was being read by his eldest son, a single red rose was dropped on to the coffin. It had been plucked from the enormous wreath sent by Lancashire County Cricket Club. Hornby's beloved wife, Ada, would survive her husband for a further two years. Today, the highly distinctive Sicilian marble sloping stone is engraved with stumps, bat and ball, plus an elegant facsimile of Hornby's highly individual and typically flamboyant signature.

Long standing team mate, Richard Barlow's oft-quoted view of his celebrated teammate was typically precise and to the point:

> First, he runs you out of breath; then he runs you out; then he gives you a sovereign; then he runs out of guineas.

He later added the following;

> A thorough gentleman, possessing good qualities all round, Lancashire are not likely to look upon his like again. They possessed in Mr Hornby one of the best captains who ever lived.

Adorned with a military style moustache, short, stocky and brimming with energy, Hornby's close cropped fair hair was neatly topped off with an immaculate centre parting. In contrast, Barlow was taller, bearded, somewhat saturnine and far more economical of movement. The first great Lancashire-born professional, he too remained an outstanding athlete. Soon renowned for his immovability, he found himself dubbed, *The Fabius Cunctator of Cricket*. Individually great players, as a pair unique, they had huge box office appeal just as county cricket was settling into a more regular rhythm. And yet, because of the game's class hierarchy at that time, each would change separately and enter the pitch from the opposite ends of the ground, only appearing together when at the crease.

Born in Barrow Bridge, Bolton, on the 28th May 1850, like Hornby, Richard Gorton Barlow was one of a large family of seven, four boys and three girls. He left school aged 14 to work in a printing office, the family later settling at Staveley in Derbyshire where he played for the local team. A genuine all-rounder, while a right-handed batsman, he also bowled left arm medium pace. He was also a talented close to the wicket fielder, renowned as a specialist at point. In June 1871, he turned out for his local team, Staveley, as they took on George Parr's All England XI. Such was his impact that a month later he was helping Lancashire overcome Yorkshire in the Roses encounter at Bramhall Lane, Sheffield. With his first ball in first class cricket he bowled Yorkshire's John West.

Batting at number six in Lancashire's first innings, Barlow ended with a resolute 28 not out. In total he carried his bat thirty times, twelve of them for Lancashire. Like W.G. Grace, he never made a first class pair. Examples of his stern obduracy abound: 17 runs in 150 minutes against Sussex in 1876, while at Liverpool he carried his bat for 44 out of 93 and then was last out, run out for 49 out of 188 in the second innings. That was against Nottinghamshire, continued victims of the Barlow barrier. In 1882, it took him eighty minutes to get off the mark as he batted right through on a difficult wicket to end with 5 not out, from a Lancashire total of 69. No wonder the exasperated Nottinghamshire bowler, William Barnes told him sternly that, *"Bowling at thee were like bowling at a stone wall!"*

Taking time to establish himself in the Lancashire side, it was 1875 before he became a regular player and 1878 before becoming a recognised bowler. His first championship century came at the Oval in 1873, as Lancashire beat Surrey by an innings and 113 runs. It was also the first time he opened the innings with A.N. Hornby. Needless to say, he was run out for a duck. In the Roses encounter at Old Trafford two years later, needing 148 to win, the pair comfortably knocked off the runs without loss, to register the first ever three figure partnership by a Lancashire opening pair. The following year in the famous encounter with Gloucestershire, while Hornby was out on his own with a splendid second innings century, as always Barlow supported solidly in a first wicket stand of 108.

One of Barlow's finest innings was undoubtedly played at Trent Bridge for the North of England against the Australian team of 1884. The North scored 91, with Barlow not out 10, the Australians replying with 100. The Australian bowler Spofforth prophesied that the Englishmen would not make 60 in their second innings. When he shot out Gunn and Bates for 53, it seemed his prophesy was coming true. Then Flowers joined Barlow and the pair added 158 for the sixth wicket. Barlow was the last out after scoring 101 in a chanceless innings that took him four and a half hours. To complete a fine all-round performance, he ended the game with match figures of 10-45. So impressed was the Australian captain, William Murdoch, that he famously took off his cap and ceremonially presented it to Barlow.

As a bowler of nagging accuracy, Barlow accounted for the great W.G. Grace more than anyone else. In the Gentlemen versus the Players encounter at the Oval in 1884, he performed the first of his three hat tricks, dismissing W.G. with the last ball one over and off the first two balls of his next over, had Shuter and Read caught at the wicket. Three years later, again for the Players against the Gentlemen, he skimmed the cream from the amateur's batting taking the wickets of W.G., Alfred Lyttleton, Hornby, A.P. Lucas, A.G. Steel, A.H. Trevor and A.H. Evans, all for a miserly 55 runs. He remains the only player to open both the batting and bowling for his country. Likewise, he is the only Lancashire player to top both the county's batting and bowling averages in the same season, that of 1882.

Barlow toured Australia three times: first under Alfred Shaw and Arthur Shrewsbury in 1881-2; secondly with Ivo Bligh's team which went on to recover The Ashes; and thirdly with Shaw and Shrewsbury in the successful tour of 1886-7. He played in every match of all three of his tours, despite an injured foot that required a runner to preserve his unique record. He even played in the famous match in San Francisco in which a baseball pitcher initially bamboozled the English batsman in the first innings before being remorselessly ill-treated in the second. Though his bowling was not enough to save the Ashes match at the Oval, his 7-40 in the third of the 1882-3 tests helped England regain the Ashes. Set to score 153 to win on a difficult wicket, not for the first time, Barlow came out on top.

In 1886, Barlow enjoyed a successful benefit game against Nottinghamshire as 10,000 spectators came to watch. Nottinghamshire donated £5.00 and with a great sense of occasion, the star of the show made 50 in three hours. Overall, he was rewarded with a return totalling in excess of £1,000. Appearing in 17 test matches, 12 of them in succession, he scored 591 runs and took 35 wickets. Between 1871 and 1891, making 249 appearances for Lancashire, he scored a total of 7,765 runs at an average of 20.38. He also took 736 wickets at an average of 13.60. His best bowling return remains 9-39 against Sussex in his benefit year. He also had 197 catches to his name. If he scored his runs more slowly than Hornby, in the end Barlow made almost as many, particularly in times of need.

While still playing for Lancashire, Barlow ran a sports outfitters business, close to Old Trafford. When Lancashire were on away games, the shop, first at Gorton House, 385 Stretford Road, then later moving closer to Victoria Station, became the focal point for supporters, its windows daubed with telegrams giving out the latest cricket scores. Always innovative, he was the first player to introduce rubber-faced gloves, single strap leg guards and removable cricket spikes. He also patented a wicket protector to help offset the vagaries of the Manchester weather. Like Hornby, Barlow was also a talented soccer player, making a number of appearances in goal for Manchester City. As a soccer referee, among the many games he officiated, undoubtedly the most famous was the first round FA Cup tie played in October 1887 at Deepdale, when Preston North End trounced Hyde United 26-0.

After his playing career wound down Barlow stayed in the game for a further twenty seasons as an umpire. He went on to become the first professional umpire to officiate in a test match. While widely respected, at one point his reputation did come under fire from the visiting Australians, unhappy with some of his decisions. While also playing on for Royton in the Central Lancashire Cricket League, together with Dick Pilling, they penned a coaching manual entitled, *Batting and Bowling with Hints on Fielding and Wicket Keeping.*[5] In 1908 came an extensive autobiography, *Forty Seasons in First Class Cricket.*[6] With forty four full page illustrations and over three hundred autographs of county cricketers, it was advertised as the autobiography and reminiscences of Richard Gorton Barlow. Inscribed on an inside page is the following: *This book is respectfully dedicated to my old and highly esteemed friend and colleague, A.N. Hornby, for many years Captain and President of the Lancashire C.C.*

That same year, having failed to settle when briefly Coach and Ground Manager at Old Trafford, Barlow, his wife Harriet and daughter, Eliza, moved to Blackpool, where they had a highly impressive double fronted villa built in Raikes View. Initially named Gorton Villa, later Alderlea, rather than a house and home, it soon became a veritable cricket museum. In the panel of the inner front door, a saintly Hornby and Barlow appeared in a stained-glass window with Dick Pilling, a gloved wicket keeper, crouching behind like a guardian angel.[7] Pictures of cricketers, past and present, adorned the impressive and rather grand entrance hall, the cavernous bathroom, rarely, if ever, able to be used for its original purpose, was increasingly used as a repository for his ever increasing collection of cricket bats and trophies. The tiled hearth in the dining room featured a picture of a cricket match, while the large window opening on the landing contained the names of all his many former team mates.

Barlow continued to run his sports goods business from his new home. When umpiring duties allowed he carried on his playing career, but now at Stanley Park with Blackpool.[8] It was there each summer that he would organise and promote popular exhibition games involving a Lancashire County XI versus an England XI. He also made a great impression when he coached the boarders at Arnold School. Having sold his impressive house to a local doctor[9], he then built a new smaller family home, Glen May, in Alderlea's once extensive back garden. There, his initials, elegantly intertwined, still proudly remain visible above the imposing front door. Living close by was his daughter, now married and with a young son christened perhaps appropriately, Leslie Barlow Wilson. In 1913, Barlow would move again, settling closer to Stanley Park in Woodland Grove. Three years earlier, despite his seemingly idyllic marriage of almost forty years, he had begun a brief affair with a local girl he met one day while out walking on the promenade. As a result, he fathered a son, Reginald Gorton Barlow Thompson.

Not enjoying the best of health in his later years, Richard Barlow crowned his life with a characteristic flourish by designing his own tombstone at Blackpool's Layton Cemetery. Topped by a head stone showing a set of stumps with the ball running through middle and leg, his epitaph modestly reads:

> Here lie the remains of Richard Gorton Barlow, died 31 July 1919, aged 68 years. For 21 seasons a playing member of the Lancashire County Cricket XI and for 21 seasons an umpire in county matches. He also made three journeys to Australia with English teams. This is a consecutive record in first class cricket which no other cricketer has achieved.

He would like to have added a great deal more of course, but sadly, there was just not enough room. Instead, inscribed lower down are just three words:

Bowled At Last.

Appendix II

LANCASHIRE
by A.N. Hornby.

Taken from The Jubilee Book of Cricket 1897

I have been requested by the author of this book to write some information regarding the history and progress of Lancashire county cricket, and to me it is a pleasure to be able to supply him with anything interesting regarding its origin. In the pavilion it has ever been customary to chronicle our club officials prominently, and from the earliest recollection that is possible to vouch for, we learn that the Manchester Club occupied some position in 1818, although when it was actually formed must be difficult to determine. In tracing the development of the old club, which undoubtedly gave birth to Lancashire, its first president, Jno. Rowlandson, who appears as far as it is possible to go back, occupied that position when the abode of the ground was in the Crescent, Salford. Little can be learned of how the game was conducted in those days, or when the members re-moved their quarters to Moss Lane, some mile and a half distant from the present Old Trafford ground; but it is certain the All- England Eleven appeared there in the forties. At all events, it is recorded that in 1842, on July 7, Manchester met the Gentlemen of the Marylebone Club at Lord's, and was practically overwhelmed; for whereas it was only able to compile 59, the Marylebone Club was credited with 220. Under these circumstances the match was not continued, and the comment was most discouraging, for it ran thus: "Conceiving they had no chance of winning, Manchester gave up the match. The bowling on the part of Manchester was very deficient, it being of the old under-hand school, which afforded the Marylebone gentle-men much amusement in hitting it away."

These were times evidently that must have been a batsman's paradise. However, as time went on, there were more successful developments, and after a long tenure the Moss Lane fields were deserted, and a new ground acquired where now stands the Botanical Gardens, almost within a stone's-throw of the present occupation. It was in September 1857 that Manchester, now a more confident and experienced team, had the assistance of Wisden, Lillywhite, and Tom Davies of Nottingham, met Surrey at Eccles, and consequent upon some fine bowling by a very old colleague of mine, Alec Rowley, it was victorious by three runs. This year the Art Treasures Exhibition was held in Manchester, and fortunately, as all future history has proved, it was arranged to be held on the cricket-ground and surroundings they occupied. This was strenuously opposed at first, but eventually amicably settled; and now, after numerous wanderings, the present site was pitched upon, and the home of the future Lancashire team, then not dreamt about as regards the high excellence of to-day, definitely decided upon.

In and around the city there was a plenitude of support, practical and financial, and the year after, 1858, nominated by Mark Phillips and seconded by T.T. Bellhouse, S.H. Swire was elected; and, as it has proved, no more excellent organiser or resourceful diplomat has guided the destinies of any club.

Then we come to the days when Broughton, Sheffield, Liverpool, and Shrewsbury provided antagonism, and here find a different class of players who retired from the game at Lord's in 1842. There were the great family of Rowleys, seven in number, whose varied abilities in every part of the game were wonderful; Joseph Makinson, one of the finest players of his time; Middlemort, Bousfield, Barber, Rev. F. Wright, who now were able to hold their own with all comers. Hereabouts also saw the ground boarded in and a pavilion raised at a cost of £900, and this sufficed until the present fine structure was erected in 1894.

The formation and progress of other county teams became an object of interest, and why Lancashire should wait, when possessed of such a grand array of players, was quickly answered with a meeting of the representatives of the various clubs held at the Queen's Hotel, Manchester, on January 12, 1864, and from that night was built up the fabric of Lancashire cricket. Those who were present on that auspicious occasion were - S.H. Swire, Frank Glover, H.W. Barber, E.B. Rowley, A.B. Rowley, D. Bleackley, T. Fothergill, Captain Ashton, A. Birley, E. Challender, J. Holt, jun., of the Manchester C.C; R.K. Birley, J. Beckton, R. Entwistle, H. Ashton, of the Western C.C.; D. Long, H. Royle, W. Horner, Higgins, of the Liverpool C.C.; J. Whittington, J.B. Payne, R. Crawshaw, F.W. Wright, of the Broughton C.C.; E. Whittaker and E. Hobson, of Ashton C.C.; J.W. Allison and E.J. Bousfield, of Longsight C.C; J. Yates, S.G. Greenwood, of Blackburn C.C.; J. Smith of Accrington; T. Wall of Wigan; J. Swailes of Oldham; Alec Eccles of Huyton; H.M. Tenent, of Northern C.C. Mr Horner was voted to the chair, while the resolution to form a county club was adopted; and on June 15, 16, 1864, the first Lancashire team appeared at Warrington to oppose Birkenhead Park Club and Ground. It was a team of amateurs, comprising the following: I. Fairclough, J. White, E.B. Rowley, J. Beacton, B.J. Lawrence, G.H. Grimshaw, S.H. Swire, J. Rowley, F.H. Gossage, W. Robinson, and T.T. Bellhouse.

The first Inter-county match was against Middlesex in July the following year, and in this Lancashire were victorious by 62 runs, this time assisted by the professionals Roger Iddison and F.R. Reynolds. The latter player I have known now and played with for many years. He was a good, steady, right-hand bowler, and became identified with the club in its infancy. He has occupied an official position almost since the club's formation, and the fine condition and excellence of the Old Trafford ground is a splendid monument to his industry and ability.

I went to Harrow in 1862, and obtained a place in the eleven in seasons 1864 and 1865, playing against Eton each year. It was in 1867 that I first played in an important match, and that was for Lancashire against Yorkshire, at Whalley, near Blackburn, in 1867. My first real connection, however, with the County Palatine began in 1869, and pleased I was at the end of that season that I had happened to obtain the highest aggregate and head the batting averages. It was in 1871 that the county unearthed two wonderful cricketers, as the sequel proves, in the persons of Barlow and Watson. Then we had Arthur Appleby, one of the finest natural left-hand bowlers I have ever seen; and with E.B. Rowley, J. Makinson, J.F. Leese, Hickton, Reynolds, and Coward, there began to combine an eleven of exceptional strength.

In 1872 the only matches Lancashire played were home and home with Derbyshire and Yorkshire, all of which engagements were won. The cricketing status of the county was now fully assured, and, progressing satisfactorily for many years, we reached our greatest ambition in 1881, when in county cricket our record was untarnished. Derbyshire, Kent, Surrey, and Yorkshire were doubly beaten, one each were won and drawn against Gloucestershire, and the only match with Middlesex was drawn. It was a triumphal season I shall ever regard with pride, for, taking part in all the matches, it was my privilege to record my first 1,000 runs in any one season. Since then Lancashire has developed in every direction in a manner altogether wonderful. I have tried to sketch its early history: that of more modern times is known to all who follow the interests of the game.

The committee are mainly composed of men who in the past liberally aided it practically and financially, and from the time, some twenty-five years back, when an annual deficit was customary, the club has been worked forward to a position of affluence. It is a matter of such dimensions now that it is more of a huge business, and when I say there are some 2800 members, whose number is continually increasing, to say nothing of some 650 ladies who take out subscription tickets, and the general management of the matches to take in hand, such an assertion will be readily understood. At Old Trafford I well remember when two professionals formed the ground staff, and to-day it is composed of 23. Inter-county fixtures have, too, increased to their highest point, and ten years ago, when Manchester, with twenty club-matches, thought it more than sufficient, there are on the list this season no fewer than seventy-nine. To accommodate thoroughly such a tremendous increase, in 1894 the new pavilion was erected, at a cost £9,100. Last season over 200,000 people passed the turnstiles, and to my mind the grounds at Old Trafford were never in better condition, or the whole club in a more healthy and flourishing position.

Perhaps I may be allowed now to say something about the men who have reared this great and lasting fabric, and whose talents lay in all directions. In its infancy what names are revered more than Mark Phillips, T.T. Bellhouse, and E. Whittaker? Then what a combination were the Rowleys, seven in number, whose cricketing abilities were of the most wonderful and varied type, and Sam Swire, Coward, Hickton, M'Intyre, and Reynolds. No finer bowler ever existed than Arthur Appleby, for with ease and grace and natural action no one could touch him. Of course there were many others a quarter of a century back whom one could dilate upon, but space forbids, and I will confine my remarks to more modern famous players. Taking them as they come first, what grand professionals Watson and Barlow were! The former for twenty-one years did wonderful service, and for length and ability to keep up there may be better, but I have not seen them. Barlow, too, was a great power, possessing all-round ability that for many years kept him in the forefront of professional cricketers. How many thousands, indeed, on both sides of the globe, witnessed poor Pilling's surprising skill! Ever on the alert, quiet, and confident, it was a sad blow to cricket generally when he was cut off in the height of a most brilliant career. Another very fine and altogether exceptional amateur was Allan Steel. Gifted all round at the wicket, or with the ball, he placed and got bowling away in a fashion peculiarly his own, and his deceptive power as a bowler troubled everybody. No better all-round man than Briggs, to sustain his form for so long, has ever represented us, and no one is known better all the world over. Very resourceful, he continues to maintain his position cleverly, and there is plenty of cricket in him yet. Walter Robinson, Nash, Crossland, Yates, and Frank Ward have all in their time rendered great service; and Messrs Frank Taylor, O.P. Lancashire, J. Eccles, S.M. Crossfield, G. Jowett, C.H. Benton, and others in the amateur division have represented it faithfully and well.

Coming to the team as at present constituted, during the last ten years no eleven has been more consistent without attaining the high position of champions. Wonderful, indeed, have been the exhibitions of Archie MacLaren. From his Harrow days up to the present he has placed on record a series of magnificent performances, at the head of which is his famous record score of 424, made against Somerset at Taunton in July 1895. Frank Sugg, Albert Ward, George Baker, and Arthur Mold are all players of the finest ability,-men who, in all the varied departments of the game, represent its truest interests, and are as well conducted as they are clever. Indeed I wish to speak in the highest terms of professional cricketers generally, who engage in a game of the most searching nature, and, by their respectfulness and respectability, make their profession one for which there is much admiration.

It would not be possible to conclude this article without referring to my excellent friend and honorary secretary, Sam Swire. First elected a member of the club in 1858, he has been in the thick of it throughout; and elected as honorary secretary in 1862, he remained until 1865, and resumed again in 1869, from which time until the present he has held uninterrupted office. He has been at the head in all its improvements and increases, and still guides it with power that few men possess.

Notes

Key to Abbreviation
W.B. - Blunt, W.S. (1919-20) *My diaries being a personal narrative of events 1888-1914. 2 vols.* London: Martin Secker.

Chapter 1
Early Days

[1] Meynell, E. (1913) *The life of Francis Thompson.* London: Burns & Oates, p.1.
[2] Hilton, J.A. (ed.) (1984) *Catholic Englishmen: essays presented to the Rt. Rev. Brian Charles Foley Bishop of Lancaster.* Wigan: North West Catholic History Society, p.45.
[3] Occurred on August 12th and 13th.
[4] Dickens, C. (1974) *Hard Times.* Oxford: Oxford University Press, p.22.
[5] Meynell, E. (1913) *The life of Francis Thompson.* London: Burns & Oates, p.10.
[6] Connolly, T.L. (1944) *Francis Thompson: in his paths. A visit to persons and places associated with the poet.* Milwaukee: Bruce Publishing Company, p.165.
[7] Boardman, B. (1988) *Between heaven and Charing Cross: the life of Francis Thompson.* New Haven: Yale University Press, p.36.
[8] Ibid, p.37.
[9] *Cassells Weekly* May 26 1923, n.p.
[10] W.B. 26th August 1907.
[11] Letter to T.L. Connolly 27th November 1937.
[12] MacKenna, R, (1932) *As shadows lengthen: the later essays of Robert W. MacKenna.* London: J. Murray
[13] Margaret Thompson died in 1954.
[14] W.B. 26th August 1907.

Chapter 2
Pitched Betwixt Heaven and Charing Cross

[1] Reid, J.C. (1959) *Francis Thompson: man and poet.* London: Routledge & Kegan Paul, p.36.
[2] Kent, W. (ed.) (1970) *An encyclopaedia of London.* Rev. ed. London: Dent, p.358.
[3] Tancred, F. (1891) 'Catholics in darkest England.' *Merry England*, 16(93), pp.172.
[4] Ibid, pp.179-180.
[5] McMaster, J. (1916) *A short history of the Royal parish of St. Martin-in-the-Fields.* London: John McMaster, p.116.
[6] Meynell, E. (1913) *The life of Francis Thompson.* London: Burns & Oates, p.76.
[7] Meynell, V. (1952) *Francis Thompson and Wilfrid Meynell: a memoir.* London:

Hollis & Carter, p.130.
[8] Lucas, E.V. (1933) *Reading, writing and remembering: a literary record.* 3rd ed. London: Methuen & Co., p.176.
[9] W.B. 26th August 1907.

Chapter 3
Storrington and Pantasaph

[1] Francis Thompson to Wilfrid Meynell letter February 1889.
[2] Vernon Blackburn 1847-1907.
[3] Boardman, B. (1988) *Between heaven and Charing Cross: the life of Francis Thompson.* New Haven: Yale University Press, p.127.
[4] Francis Thompson to Canon Carroll letter November 1889.
[5] Meynell, E. (1913) *The life of Francis Thompson.* London: Burns & Oates., p.96.
[6] Walsh, J. (1968) *Strange harp, strange symphony: the life of Francis Thompson.* London: W.H. Allen, p.107.
[7] Francis Thompson to Wilfrid Meynell letter 4th January 1893.
[8] Kenealy, A, (1933) *'Francis Thompson: the man and his poetry.'* The Capuchin Annual, p.39.
[9] Meynell, E. (1913) The life of Francis Thompson. London: Burns & Oates, p.187.
[10] Francis Thompson to Alice Meynell letter June 1896.
[11] Letter from Norbert Thompson to John Walsh 2nd July 1964.

Chapter 4
The Hound of Heaven

[1] The Hound of Heaven first published in Poems in 1893.
[2] Reid, J.C. (1959) *Francis Thompson: man and poet.* London: Routledge & Kegan Paul, pp.82-87.
[3] Published Viking Press 1940.
[4] Published F.A. Thorpe 1972.
[5] Published Pocket Books 1952.
[6] Television Broadcast 1989.
[7] Published Geoffrey Bles1933.
[8] Published Kingsway 1982.
[9] Published Chatto and Windus 1914.
[10] Published Mowbrays 1947.
[11] Sequence of 23 paintings entitled *A Pictorial Sequence Painted by R.H. Ives Gammell Based on The Hound of Heaven* 1941-1956.
[12] Held on May 17th 1936.
[13] Published by Stainer Bell 1920.
[14] Holst composed choral settings of *Dream Tryst* and *Sister Songs.*
[15] *BBC Music Magazine*, December 2017.
[16] Published J. Curwen & Sons Ltd.

[17] Cawood, I. (2015) 'Don't let me go! Hold me down!: inspiration, voice and image in Kate Bush's Hounds of Love.' *Popular Music*, 35(1) pp.41-63.
[18] *The Gramophone*, June 1971, p.58.
[19] Performed 27th October at The National Shine of the Immaculate Conception.
[20] Published Highbridge Music 1980.
[21] Burne-Jones, E. (1904) *Memorials of Edward Burne-Jones*. London: Macmillan, p.240.
[22] Wavell, A.P. (1944) *Other men's flowers: an anthology of poetry*. London: Jonathan Cape, p.8.

Chapter 5
Poetry and Prose

[1] 12th November 1893.
[2] Composed 1956.
[3] Meynell, E. (1913) *The life of Francis Thompson*. London: Burns & Oates, p.150.
[4] Jackson, H. (1976) *The eighteen nineties: a review of art and ideas at the close of the nineteenth century*. Hassocks: Harvester Press, p.51.
[5] Mégroz, R.L. (1927) *Francis Thompson: the poet of earth in heaven*. London: Faber & Gwyer, p.219.
[6] Walsh, J. (1968) *Strange harp, strange symphony: the life of Francis Thompson*. London: W.H. Allen, p.277.
[7] *New Poems* published 1897.
[8] Ibid.
[9] Coventry Patmore died 26th November 1896.
[10] *New Poems* published 1897.
[11] Lees, F.N. (1960) 'Francis Thompson: 1859-1907'. *Bulletin of the John Rylands Library* Manchester, 42(2) pp.388.
[12] Thompson, F. (1902) 'Cecil Rhodes.' *The Academy*, 1562 April 12th, p.378.
[13] Meynell, E. (1913) *The life of Francis Thompson*. London: Burns & Oates, p.225.
[14] Ibid p.160.
[15] Connolly, T.L. (1948) *Literary criticisms by Francis Thompson*. Westport, CT: Greenwood Press, p.viii.
[16] Ibid, ix.
[17] Butter, P.H. (1961) *Francis Thompson*. London: Longmans, p.19.
[18] Danchin, P. (1959) *Francis Thompson: la vie et l'oeuvre d'un poéte*. Paris: A0G. Nizet.
[19] Boston College Notebook 117.
[20] Boston College Notebook 23.
[21] Thompson, F. (1899) 'Book review.' *The Academy* 17th June.
[22] Boston College Notebook 40.
[23] Thompson, F (1909) *Shelley: an essay*. London: Burns & Oates.

Chapter 6
Cricketana

[1] Lucas, E.V. (1908) 'Francis Thompson's cricket verses.' *The Cornhill Magazine*, 25 (July) pp.58.
[2] Ibid p.58-59.
[3] Boardman, B. (2001) *The poems of Francis Thompson*. New ed. London: Continuum, p.488.
[4] Connolly, T.L. (1944) *Francis Thompson: in his paths. A visit to persons and places associated with the poet*. Milwaukee: Bruce Publishing Company.
[5] John Hornby 1887-1927.

Chapter 7
The Field is Full of Shades

[1] Ghosh, S.K. (1909) *The prince of destiny*. S.l.: Redman, p.191.
[2] Walsh, J. (1968) *Strange harp, strange symphony: the life of Francis Thompson*. London: W.H. Allen, p.189.
[3] W.B. 26th August 1907.
[4] Monroe, H. (1938) *A poet's life*. New York: Macmillan, pp.148-149.
[5] Meynell, V. (1952) *Francis Thompson and Wilfrid Meynell: a memoir*. London: Hollis & Carter.
[6] Meynell, V. (1929) *Alice Meynell: a memoir*. London: Burns Oates and Washbourne & Jonathan Cape.
[7] Poems are entitled *Threaten Tears*, *Arab Love Song*, *Buona Notte* and *The Passion of Mary*.
[8] Meynell, E. (1913) *The life of Francis Thompson*. London: Burns & Oates.
[9] W.B. 26th August 1907.
[10] Whitten, W. (1907) 'Francis Thompson.' *T.P.'s Weekly*, 29th November, p.696.
[11] Meynell, A. (1908) 'Some memories of Francis Thompson.' *Dublin Review*, 142 (284/285) pp.160-172.
[12] Meynell, E. (1913) *The life of Francis Thompson*. London: Burns & Oates, p.351.
[13] Thomson, J. (1912) *Francis Thompson: the Preston-born poet*. Preston: Alfred Halewood, p.1.
[14] Meynell, E. (1913) *The life of Francis Thompson*. London: Burns & Oates, p.350.
[15] Connolly, T.L. (1944) *Francis Thompson: in his paths. A visit to persons and places associated with the poet*. Milwaukee: Bruce Publishing Company.
[16] Connolly, T.L. (ed.) (1957) *The man has wings: new poems and plays by Francis Thompson*. New York: Hanover House.
[17] In 1976, the American composer Emma Lou Diemer(born 1927) set four of Alice's poems for soprano, tenor, two flutes, piccolo, two percussion, vibraphone, xylophone, harp, harpsichord, piano and strings.
[18] Tynan, K. (1910) 'Francis Thompson.' *Fortnightly Review*, 87(518) pp.349.
[19] Chesterton, G.K. (1913) *The Victorian age in literature*. London: Thornton

Butterworth, p.202-203.
[20] Sir Francis Meynell Address 21st January 1967.

Appendix I
O My Hornby And My Barlow Long Ago!

[1] Lucas, E.V. (1908) 'Francis Thompson's cricket verses.' *The Cornhill Magazine*, 25 (July) pp.58-66.
[2] Boardman, B. (2001) *The poems of Francis Thompson*. New ed. London: Continuum.
[3] Lancashire 1874-1882.
[4] Published 1887.
[5] Published 1900.
[6] Published 1908.
[7] Now on show in the Pavilion at Old Trafford Cricket Ground.
[8] Barlow Crescent now proudly fronts Blackpool Cricket Club, while in Manchester just five hundred yards north of Old Trafford Cricket Ground, Barlow Road and Hornby Road are yet further reminders of this intrepid duo.
[9] Robert Dunderdale

Bibliography

Works of Frances Thompson

Tancred, F. (1891) 'Catholics in darkest England.' *Merry England*, 16(93), pp.171-187.

Thompson, F. (1893) *Poems*. London: Elkin Matthew and John Lane.

Thompson, F. (1895) *Sister songs: an offering to two sisters*. London: John Lane.

Thompson, F. (1897) *New poems*. London: Constable.

Thompson, F. (1897) 'A prince of India on the prince of games.' *The Academy*, 1322 pp.175-176.

Thompson, F. (1908) 'Shelley.' *Dublin Review*, 143(286/287) pp, 25-49.

Thompson, F (1909) *Shelley: an essay*. London: Burns & Oates.

Thompson, F. (1909) *St. Ignatius Loyola*. London: Burns & Oates.

Thompson, F. (1911) *The life and labours of St. John Baptists de la Salle*. London: Burns & Oates.

Thompson, F. and Connolly, T.L. (1948) *Literary criticisms*. New York: E.P. Dutton.

Collections of Francis Thompson Poetry

Meynell, W. (ed.) (1908) *Selected poems of Francis Thompson*. London: Burns, Oates and Methuen.

Meynell, W. (ed.) (1913) *The works of Francis Thompson*. 3 vols. London: Burns & Oates.

Shorter, C. (ed.) (1917) *The Uncollected Verses by Francis Thompson*. Privately Printed.

Connolly, T.L. (ed.) (1941) *The poems of Francis Thompson*. Rev. ed., New York: D. Appleton-Century Company.

Thompson, F. (1946) *The poems of Francis Thompson*. London: Hollis & Carter.

Connolly, T.L. (ed.) (1957) *The man has wings: new poems and plays by Francis Thompson*. New York: Hanover House.

Boardman, B. (2001) *The poems of Francis Thompson*. New ed. London: Continuum.

Music Scores

Blake, H. (2005) *Benedictus: vocal score*. London: Highbridge Music.

Corp, R. (2009) *The Hound of Heaven: poem by Francis Thompson*. Unknown place of publication: Ronald Corp.

Harris, W. (1920) *The Hound of Heaven: poem by Francis Thompson – set to music for baritone solo, chorus & orchestra*. London: Stainer & Bell Ltd.

Jacobson, M. (n.d.) *The Hound of Heaven: for tenor solo, S.A.T.B. and orchestra*. London: J. Curwen & Sons Ltd.

Other Sources

Anonymous (1894) 'Review of Poems by Francis Thompson.' *The Athenaeum*, 3rd February pp.143-144.

Anonymous (1896) 'Recent poetry.' *Edinburgh Review*, 376 (April) pp.493-502.

Anonymous (1909) 'Review of Selected Poems.' *The Athenaeum*, 4237 pp.37-38.
Anonymous (1909) 'Williams Barnes and Francis Thompson.' *Contemporary Review*, 95(19) pp.19-21.
Anonymous (1913) 'Francis Thompson and the Academy: review of the works of Francis Thompson.' *The Academy*, 2145 pp.745-746.
Anonymous (1913) 'The story of a poet: review of the life of Francis Thompson by Everard Meynell.'. *The Academy*, 2169, pp.682-683.
Anonymous (1958) 'The Hound of Heaven.' *Music Teacher*, March, p.139.
Badeni, J. (1981) *The slender tree: a life of Alice Meynell*. Padstow: Tabb House.
Bailey, P, Thorn, P. and Wynne-Tomas, P. (1993) *Who's who of cricketers*. Rev ed. London: Hamlyn.
Barlow, R.G. (1900) *Batting and bowling: with hints on fielding and wicket-keeping*. London: Geo G. Bussey & Co.
Barlow, R.G. (1908) *Forty seasons of first class cricket: being the autobiography and reminiscences of Richard Gorton Barlow*. Manchester: John Heywood Ltd.
Barnett, R. (2009) 'Ronald Corp: The Hound of Heaven'. *BMS News*, 124 pp.239-240.
Barry, W. (1910) 'Francis Thompson's life of St. Ignatius'. *Dublin Review*, 147(294/295) pp.56-84.
Bearshaw, B. (1990) *From the Streford end: the official history of Lancashire County Cricket Club*. London: Partridge Press.
Beck, G.A. (1950) *The English Catholics 1850-1950: essays to commemorate the centenary of the restoration of the hierarchy of England and Wales*. London: Burns & Oates.
Begg, P. (2004) *Jack the Ripper: the facts*. London: Robson.
Berridge, V. (1981) *Opium and the people: opiate use in the nineteenth-century England*. London: Allen Lane.
Blunt, W.S. (1907) 'Francis Thompson.' *The Academy*, 1855, pp.164-165.
Blunt, W.S. (1919-20) *My diaries being a personal narrative of events 1888-1914*. 2 vols. London: Martin Secker.
Boardman, B. (1988) *Between heaven and Charing Cross: the life of Francis Thompson*. New Haven: Yale University Press.
Brodkin, S. (2007) *Johnny Briggs: poor Johnny*. Cardiff: Association of Cricket Statisticians and Historians.
Brodkin, S. (2013) *A.N. Hornby: the boss*. Cardiff: Association of Cricket Statisticians and Historians.
Buchen, I.H. (1964) 'Source-hunting versus tradition: Francis Thompson's The Hound of Heaven.' *Victorian Poetry*, 2(2) pp.111-115.
Buchen. I.H. (1965) 'Francis Thompson and the aesthetics of the incarnation'. *Victorian Poetry*, 3(4) pp.235-244.
Burdett, O. (1925) *The Beardsley period: an essay in perspective*. London: John Lane.
Burne-Jones, E. (1904) *Memorials of Edward Burne-Jones*. London: Macmillan.
Butter, P.H. (1961) *Francis Thompson*. London: Longmans.
Colum, P., Meynell, F., and Chesterton, C.K. (1910) *Eyes of youth: a book of verse*.

London: Herbert & Daniel.
Cawood, I. (2015) 'Don't let me go! Hold me down!: inspiration, voice and image in Kate Bush's Hounds of Love.' *Popular Music*, 35(1) pp.41-63.
Chesterton, G.K. (1913) *The Victorian age in literature.* London: Thornton Butterworth.
Chesterton, G.K. (1951) *Selected essays.* London: Methuen.
Connolly, T.L. (ed.) (1937) *An account of books and manuscripts of Francis Thompson.* Chestnut Hill, Mass: Boston College.
Connolly, T.L. (1944) *Francis Thompson: in his paths. A visit to persons and places associated with the poet.* Milwaukee: Bruce Publishing Company.
Connolly, T.L. (1948) *Literary criticisms by Francis Thompson.* Westport, CT: Greenwood Press.
De la Mare, W. (1953) *Private view.* London: Faber & Faber.
Erpelding, M.W. (2014) *'The danger of the disappearance of things': William Henry Harris The Hound of Heaven.* DMA. University of Iowa.
Evans, I. (1966) *English poetry in the later nineteenth century.* 2nd revised ed., London: Methuen.
Finberg, H.P.R. (1925) 'Francis Thompson.' *The English Review,* 12(6) pp.822-831.
Fogey, A. (1894) 'The young men.' *The Contemporary Review*, 65 pp.177-188.
Frewin, L. (ed.) 1964) *The poetry of cricket: an anthology.* London: Macdonald.
Graves, R. (1949) *The common Asphodel: collected essays on poetry.* London: Hamish Hamilton.
Green, D. (1990) *The history of Gloucestershire County Cricket Club.* London: Christopher Helm.
Green, S. (1997) 'My Hornby & my Barlow of a very long time ago now'. *The Cricketer,* April p.28.
Harding, G. (1988) *Opiate addiction, morality and medicine: from moral illness to pathological disease.* Basingstoke: Macmillan.
Harrison, A. (1913) 'The poetry of Francis Thompson.' *The English Review*, 15(1), pp.103-116.
Hayhurst, K. (2016) *The story of a cricket stained glass window.* Stockport: Keith Hayhurst.
Hayter, A. (1968) *Opium and the romantic imagination.* London: Faber & Faber.
Henderson, J. and Jervis, T. (2018) *Sir William Henry Harris: organist, choir trainer and composer.* Salisbury: The Royal School of Church Music.
Hill, T.H. (2016) 'John Hornby: legend or fool'. *Torch Magazine*, Winter pp.6-9.
Hilton, J.A. (ed.) (1984) *Catholic Englishmen: essays presented to the Rt. Rev. Brian Charles Foley Bishop of Lancaster.* Wigan: North West Catholic History Society.
Hind, C.L. (1927) 'Francis Thompson: another book.' *The Bookman*, 72(429), pp.164-165.
Hodcroft, G.A. (1984) *My own red roses.* Lewes: Book Guild.
Hole, W.G. (1908) 'Francis Thompson: in memoriam'. *Dublin Review*, 143(286/287) pp.274-277.
Hoole, W.H. (1991) *The cricketing squire.* Clapham: Writers Own Publications.

Jackson, H. (1976) *The eighteen nineties: a review of art and ideas at the close of the nineteenth century*. Hassocks: Harvester Press.
Jacobson, J. (2007) 'The music of Maurice Jacobson'. *BMS News*, 115 pp.198-205.
J.W.B. (1922) 'Review of Lebuffe's study of The Hound of Heaven.' *Modern Language Notes*, 37(2) pp.124-128.
Kavanagh, P.J. (1985) 'Mr Hornby and Barlow'. *The Spectator*, 255(8195) pp.33-34.
Kay, J. (1972) *Lancashire: a history of county cricket*. London: Arthur Barker.
Kenealy, A, (1933) 'Francis Thompson: the man and his poetry.' *The Capuchin Annual*, pp.39-59.
Kent, W. (ed.) (1970) *An encyclopaedia of London*. Rev. ed. London: Dent.
Lancashire County Cricket Club (1984) *The Old Trafford story 1884-1984*. Chorley: Nelson Brothers Printers.
Lang, A. (1894) 'The young men.' *Contemporary Review*, 65 pp.177-188.
LeBuffe, F.P. (1922) *The Hound of Heaven: an interpretation*. New York: The Macmillan Company.
Ledbrooke, A.W. (1954) *Lancashire county cricket: the official history of the Lancashire county & Manchester cricket club 1864-1953*. London: Phoenix House.
Lees, F.N. (1960) 'Francis Thompson: 1859-1907'. *Bulletin of the John Rylands Library Manchester*, 42(2) pp.378-394.
Longford, E. (1979) *A pilgrimage of passion: the life of Wilfrid Scawen Blunt*. London: Weidenfeld and Nicolson.
Lucas, A. (1939) *E.V. Lucas: a portrait*. London: Methuen and Co.
Lucas, E.V. (1908) 'Francis Thompson's cricket verses.' *The Cornhill Magazine*, 25(July) pp.58-66.
Lucas, E.V. (1989) *Cricket all his life: the cricket writings of E.V. Lucas*. London: Pavilion Library.
Marshall, J. (1973) *Old Trafford*. Newton Abbot: Sportsman Book Club.
McCourt, E. (1967) *Remember Butler: the story of Sir William Butler*. London: Routledge & Kegan Paul.
MacKenzie, R. (2002) *A critical biography of English novelist Viola Meynell, 1885-1956*. Lewiston, N.Y.: Edwin Mellen Press.
Mégroz, R.L. (1927) *Francis Thompson: the poet of earth in heaven*. London: Faber & Gwyer.
Meredith, A. and Harris, P. (2007) *Malcolm Williamson: a mischievous muse*. London: Omnibus Press.
Meynell, A. (1908) 'Some memories of Francis Thompson.' *Dublin Review*, 142(284/285)pp.160-172.
Meynell, A., Page, F., Meynell, F.M.W., Stokes, A., Ellis, T. and Sackville-West, V. (1947) *Prose and poetry: centenary volume*. London: Cape.
Meynell, E. (1913) *The life of Francis Thompson*. London: Burns & Oates.
Meynell, E. (1916) *The life of Francis Thompson*. New ed., London: Burns & Oates.
Meynell, F. (1971) *My lives*. London: The Bodley Head.
Meynell, V. (1929) *Alice Meynell: a memoir*. London: Burns Oates and Washbourne & Jonathan Cape.

Meynell, V. (1952) *Francis Thompson and Wilfrid Meynell: a memoir*. London: Hollis & Carter.
Meynell, W. (1907) 'Mr. Francis Thompson.' *The Athenaeum*, 4178) pp.654-656.
Meynell, W. (ed.) (1937) *Francis Thompson: poetical works*. Oxford: Oxford University Press.
Midwinter, E. (1989) *Red roses crest the caps: the story of Lancashire county cricket club*. London: Kingswood Press.
Milligan, B. (2005) 'Morphine-addicted doctors, the English opium-eater, and embattled medical authority.' *Victorian Literature and Culture*, 33(2) pp.541-553.
Patmore, C. (1894) 'Mr. F. Thompson, a new poet.' *Fortnightly Review*, 55(325) pp.19-24.
Patmore, D. (1939 *The life and times of Coventry Patmore*. London: Constable.
Pelly, D.F. (2002) 'The legend of John Hornby: a Thelon river tale.' *Above & Beyond*, November/December pp.30-31, 33, 35, 37, 39.
Plant, S. (2001) *Writing on drugs*. London: Faber & Faber.
Pogson, R. (1952) *Lancashire county cricket*. London: Convoy Publications.
Powell, A.G. and Canynge Caple, S. (1974) *The Graces (E.M., W.G. & G.F.)*. Bath: Chivers.
Ranjitsinhji, K.S. (1897) *The jubilee book of cricket*. Edinburgh: Blackwood & Sons.
Reid, J.C. (1959) *Francis Thompson: man and poet*. London: Routledge & Kegan Paul.
Rogerson, I. (1979) *Sir Francis Meynell and the Nonesuch Press*. Manchester: Manchester Polytechnic Library.
Rogerson, I. (1992) *Sir Francis Meynell: designer extraordinary*. London: Nonesuch Press.
Ross, A. (1983) *Ranji: prince of cricketers*. London: Collins.
Scholes, P.A. (1921) *New works by modern British composers*. London: Stainer & Bell.
Searle, A., Edwards, P., Hardcastle, G. and Lorimer, M.G. (2014) *150 years of Lancashire cricket: 1864-2014*. Nantwich; Max Books.
Standing, P.C. (1924) 'Cricket in fiction and poetry.' *The English Review*, June pp.868-875.
Stevens, T.H.G. (1958) *Manchester of yesterday*. Altrincham: Sherratt.
Symons, A. (1894) 'Review of Poems by Francis Thompson.' *The Athenaeum*, 3458 pp.143-144.
Thompson, F. (1947) *The Hound of Heaven: with decorations by Jean Young*. London: A.R. Mowbray & Co.
Thompson, F. and Connolly, T.L. (1948) Literary criticisms. [1st ed.] ed., New York: E.P. Dutton.
Thomson, A.A. (1958) *Odd men in: a gallery of cricket eccentrics*. London: Museum Press.
Thomson, A.A. (1967) *Cricket: the wars of the roses*. London: Pelham Books.
Thomson, G.R. (1894) 'Review: poems by Francis Thompson.' *The Academy*, 1145, pp.302-303.

Thomson, J. (1912) *Francis Thompson: the Preston-born poet*. Preston: Alfred Halewood.
Thomson, P. van K. (1961) *Francis Thompson: a critical biography*. New York: Thomas Nelson & Sons.
Tomlinson, R. (2015) *Amazing grace: the man who was W.G.* London: Little, Brown.
Tynan, K. (1910) 'Francis Thompson.' *Fortnightly Review*, 87(518) pp.349-360.
Tynan, K. (1913) 'Francis Thompson: the master of vision.' *The Bookman*, 44(263) pp.208-210.
Tynan, K. (1918) 'Francis Thompson.' *The Bookman*, 54(321) pp.87-89.
Waldron, R. (1999) *The Hound of Heaven at my heels: the lost diary of Francis Thompson*. San Francisco: Ignatius Press.
Walsh, J. (1968) *Strange harp, strange symphony: the life of Francis Thompson*. London: W.H. Allen.
Walsh, J, (ed.) (1969) *The letters of Francis Thompson*. New York: Hawthorn Books Inc.
Wavell, A.P. (1944) *Other men's flowers: an anthology of poetry*. London: Jonathan Cape.
Whalley, G. (1962) *The legend of John Hornby*. London: John Murray.
Whitten, W. (1907) 'Francis Thompson.' *T.P.'s Weekly*, 29th November, p.696.
Wright, G. (1983) 'Francis Thompson in all of us.' *Wisden Cricket Monthly*, July pp.33-34.
Wynne-Thomas, P. (1989) *The history of Lancashire County Cricket Club*. London: Christopher Helm.

Also consulted were various volumes of *Oxford Dictionary of National Biography*, *Wisden Cricketer' Almanack*, *Who's Who* and *Who Was Who* and assorted newspaper articles.

Index

Picture credits

Plate section one
Francis Thompson Photograph 1894 (Cover)
Dr Charles Thompson Photograph 1877
Mary Thompson Photograph 1877
Francis Thompson with his Sisters Photograph 1870
Annie Thompson Photograph 1887
Preston Marketplace Drawing 1859
7 Winckley Street, Preston Photograph
Stamford Street, Ashton-under-Lyne Postcard
Francis Thompson Photograph 1874
Lafcadio Hearn Photograph
Ushaw College Drawing 1870
Admission Register, Manchester Royal Infirmary 1878
Francis Thompson Photograph 1898
Illustrations by Gustave Doré from the Jerrold, B. and Doré (1872) *London: a pilgrimage*. London: Grant and Co.
Alice and Wilfrid Meynell (Courtesy of the Meynell Family)

Plate section two
Meynell Family at Palace Court (Courtesy of the Meynell Family)
Alice Meynell (Courtesy of the Meynell Family)
47 Palace Court, Bayswater (Courtesy of the Meynell Family)
Storrington Priory Photograph 1891
Creccas Cottage at Pantasaph Photograph 1895
Maggie and Agnes Brien Photograph 1895
Coventry Patmore Photograph 1894
Katie King (Courtesy of the Meynell Family)
First publication of *The Hound of Heaven* in *Merry England*. Covers of published poetry.
E.V. Lucas (Courtesy of the Meynell Family)
Everard Meynell (Courtesy of the Meynell Family)
Cover of *The Life of Francis Thompson* by Everard Meynell
Maurice Jacobson (Courtesy of Julian Jacobson)
Fartein Valen (Courtesy of British Music Society)
Sir William Harris (Courtesy of Robert Eggar)
Howard Blake (Courtesy of Howard Blake)
The Hound of Heaven Music Cover

Ronald Corp (Courtesy of Ronald Corp)
Francis Thompson, sketch by Everard Meynell, 1907
Francis Thompson Will 1907
Memorial Plaque, Manchester, Carved by Eric Gill (Author's Collection)
Francis Thompson's grave at Kensal Green Cemetery (Author's Collection)
Memorial Plaque, Harris Museum, Preston (Author's Collection)

Plate section three
A.N. Hornby (Courtesy of Harrow School)
R. G Barlow (Author's Collection)
Lancashire County Champions, 1881 (Courtesy of Lancashire County Cricket Club)
Stained glass window R.G. Barlow, Dick Pilling and A.N. Hornby (Author's Collection)
R.G. Barlow pediment (Author's Collection)
R. G. Barlow houses, Alderlea and Glen May, Raikes Parade, Blackpool (Author's Collection)
A.N. Hornby portrait and grave (Author's Collection)
R.G. Barlow portrait and grave (Author's Collection)
W.G. Grace Photograph 1883
K.S. Ranjitsinhji Photograph 1901
Fuller Pilch Print 1845
Old Trafford Pavilion, 1868 (Courtesy of Lancashire County Cricket Club)
A.H. Hornby (Courtesy of Lancashire County Cricket Club)
Dick Pilling (Courtesy of Lancashire County Cricket Club)

Author's portrait (Courtesy of Rob Lock)

Every effort has been made to contact all copyright holders. The author would be pleased to make good in future editions any errors or omissions.

About the Author

Fast approaching half a century of active involvement in the world of cricket, be it as a player, umpire and administrator, Kenneth Shenton's earliest memories of the game are of his father opening the bowling for his local team, Nantwich, at that time based on The Barony, and playing a leading role in the life of The North Staffs and South Cheshire Cricket League. Astutely captained as always by their legendary and long serving wicket keeper, Geoff Bull, at that time the runs constantly flowed from the bat of the club's revered Indian test star, Gulabrai Sipahimalani Ramchand.

Born, like his father, in the same small Cheshire market town, Kenneth Shenton was educated at Edleston Road Primary School and Nantwich and Acton Grammar School. While there he studied the organ with the distinguished and long serving Organist of St Mary's Parish Church, Harold Kirkham. He then went on to read music at the University of London, before undertaking postgraduate studies at Keble College, Oxford. After teaching locally for some years, he then spent some thirty three years as Director of Music at one of the north west's leading independent schools.

As a writer, a regular contributor to publications as diverse as *The Cricketer* and *The Church Times*, he also compiles obituaries for the national press, as well as The Professional Cricketers' Association. As a broadcaster, he has both written and narrated numerous documentary programmes across the air waves. These include everything from Promenade Concert interval talks on Radio Three, *The Resort Without Peer* on Radio Two and, on Radio Four, a centenary tribute to the eminent musicologist and composer, Elizabeth Poston, intriguingly titled *Tinker, Tailor, Composer, Spy*. His publications range from *The Songs of C.B. Rootham* to *The Complete Organ Works of Basil Harwood*.

Married with two daughters, he lives on the Fylde Coast.